Twayne's English Authors Series

Sylvia E. Bowman, *Editor*

INDIANA UNIVERSITY

Forrest Reid

TEAS 199

Forrest Reid

FORREST REID

By **MARY BRYAN**
Regis College

TWAYNE PUBLISHERS

A DIVISION OF G. K. HALL & CO., BOSTON

Copyright © 1976 by G.K. Hall & Co.
All Rights Reserved
First Printing

Library of Congress Cataloging in Publication Data

Bryan, Mary, 1922–
  Forrest Reid.

  (Twayne's English authors series; TEAS 199)
  Bibliography: p.
  Includes index.
  1. Reid, Forrest, 1875–1947.   2.   Novelists, Irish—
20th century—Biography.
PR6035.E43Z59   823'.9'12   76-48210
ISBN 0-8057-6661-8

To Professors Edward Wagenknecht and
Grace A. Hawley for their inspiration and
friendship "down the days."

Contents

About the Author

Preface

Chronology

1. A Portrait of the Artist   15

2. The Literary Milieu   32

3. Pipes of Pan in Belfast: The Early Novels (1904–1912)   54

4. I Too Was in Arcadia: The Middle Period (1913–1922)   83

5. The Milk of Paradise: The Major Novels (1927–1947)   114

6. Conclusion   144

    Notes and References   151

    Selected Bibliography   161

    Index   167

About the Author

Mary Bryan is currently head of the Department of English, professor of English, and co-director of Women's Studies at Regis College, a liberal arts college for women located in Weston, Massachusetts. She conducts seminars on the modern novel, literary criticism, Romanticism, and Women and the Art of Fiction. She has served on the Massachusetts State Conference of the American Association of University Professors on the Academic Freedom and Tenure Committee. She has lectured to teachers' groups on sexism in language and literature. At the Thomas Crane Library in Quincy, Massachusetts, she has in the past led adult group discussions on modern and contemporary fiction. At the Modern Language Association Convention in New York in 1974, at the seminar on May Sarton, she presented the conclusions of her monograph "Rage for Justice: Selected Novels of May Sarton," which was printed in abstracts of *PMLA* and *Women's Studies*, 1975. In addition to her interest in civil rights, she lists her main interests as reading, drama, music, and gardening.

She received her A. B. degree from Regis College in 1944 and her M. A. and Ph.D. degrees from Boston University in 1945 and 1959. She studied under Professors Edward Wagenknecht and Gerald Warner Brace. From 1948–54, she taught the modern novel in the evening division of Adult Education for the Massachusetts Division of University Extension. From 1955–56 she was a Fulbright scholar at the University of Munich, where she studied the influence of German criticism on American literary critics. Professor Bryan is now working on Forrest Reid's criticism and book reviews, and continuing her work on May Sarton. She has recently contributed an article entitled "Vision and Dreams: The *Tom Barber* Trilogy," for an anniversary edition of *Threshold*, an Ulster literary periodical, in honor of Forrest Reid.

Preface

The purpose of this critical study of Forrest Reid's novels is to indicate this author's significance as a psychological novelist whose explorations of multilevel reality through the eyes of sensitive, imaginative, exceptional boys deserve a wider reading public than they have heretofore reached. A modern Romantic Hellenist who chose Greece as his imaginary kingdom, Reid's dedication to humane values in a world of war, violence, and political tyrannies is a quiet, minority voice in twentieth-century fiction.

My interest in the novels of Forrest Reid began because of a statement in Professor Edward Wagenknecht's "Appendix" to his *Cavalcade of the English Novel* that "Reid is one of the most outstanding individualists among contemporary British novelists, and, in America at least, one of the most unjustly neglected" (568–69). As an Anglo-Irish novelist, Reid's relevancy today is for his visionary idealism and for his persistent concern for human rights that are evident throughout his works.

I have drawn extensively upon Reid's two autobiographies, *Apostate* and *Private Road*, since they are important documents; for they are basic to an understanding of not only his quarrel with Christianity but also his acceptance of the Greek way as his guide to spiritual values. Likewise, the pioneer study by Russell Burlingham entitled *Forrest Reid: A Portrait and a Study*, with an introduction by Walter de la Mare, is an invaluable critical source for the light it sheds on Reid as a person and as a significant prose stylist.

This book is divided into six chapters. Chapter 1, which treats Reid's life from his autobiographies, adds information from historical and biographical sources in order to understand his self-image and his Hellenism, as well as to set the background for an interpretation of his novels. Chapter 2 contains the intellectual and cultural milieu in European thought to which Reid belongs, his similarity to E.M. Forster, and his ideas on the lyrical novel. Chapters 3, 4, and 5 discuss Reid's novels in chronological sequence as Reid suggested in *Brian Westby* in order to show the ideal that each novel expresses. Chapter 6 considers Reid's relevance and significance as a modern psychological novelist and as a critic whose style expresses his individuality. In a study of this length, it is not possible to treat more fully the stature of Reid as a literary critic or to include as many narrative passages to illustrate Reid's style as might otherwise be possible. The fact that his novels are difficult to procure suggests the need for his major fiction, at least, to be printed in paperback editions so that readers may experience the unique quality of his mind and style from primary sources.

Since the rights to Forrest Reid's works have reverted to his heir, Mr. Stephen Gilbert, Reid's friend and literary executor, I am deeply grateful for his permission to quote from the literature of Reid published by the following: Ernest Benn, Ltd., *The Kingdom of Twilight* and *Pirates of the Spring;* Edward Arnold, Ltd., *The Bracknels, Following Darkness, The Gentle Lover, At the Door of the Gate, The Spring Song;* William Collins and Sons, Ltd. for *Pender Among the Residents* and *Demophon;* Faber and Faber, Ltd. for *Uncle Stephen, Brian Westby, The Retreat, Young Tom, Denis Bracknel, Peter Waring, Apostate, Private Road, Retrospective Adventures,* and Russell Burlingham's *Forrest Reid: A Portrait and a Study;* and Pantheon Books, Inc. (Random House) for the *Tom Barber* trilogy (*Young Tom, The Retreat,* and *Uncle Stephen*).

I wish to thank the librarians and staff of the Regis College library, Weston, Massachusetts, for arranging interlibrary loans; the library of the University of Wisconsin for allowing me the use of a copy of *The Garden God;* the University of Illinois library for a like use of Reid's novel *Demophon;* the Harvard College library for a copy of *Pirates of the Spring;* and Professor Edward Wagenknecht for the loan of his personal copy of *The Kingdom of Twilight.* I am grateful to the staff of the Boston Public Library, and of the Thomas Crane Public Library, Quincy, Massachusetts, as also to Mr. R. M. Jenkinson of the Central Library, Belfast, for a copy of the *Forrest Reid Catalogue.* For information regarding Reid's school days, I am indebted to Mr. L. F. Washbrook, registrar of The Royal Academical Institution, Belfast, and also for a copy of *School News* for Easter, 1947, containing two articles on Forrest Reid. I wish to express my thanks to Mr. D. Webster, clerk of the tutors, Christ's College, Cambridge, England, for the information that enabled me to arrive at the exact date of Forrest Reid's entrance to Cambridge University; to Canon R. A. Deane, St. Thomas' Rectory, Belfast, for his letter confirming the early church affiliation of Forrest Reid; and to the British Broadcasting Corporation for a copy of a talk on Forrest Reid shortly after his death given by the Honorable John Sparrow.

To Professors Edward Wagenknecht and Gerald Warner Brace, both emeriti of Boston University; to my colleague and friend Professor Grace Hawley, emerita of Regis College, Weston, Massachusetts; and to the trustees of Regis College and Sister Jeanne d'Arc O'Hare, fifth president, for a sabbatical leave that enabled me to bring this study to fruition, I now express my gratitude. Finally, to Sylvia E. Bowman for her excellent advice and for her careful editing of this text I am most grateful.

MARY BRYAN

Regis College
Weston, Mass.

Chronology

1875   Forrest Reid born in Belfast, Ireland, on June 24.

1884   Attended Miss Hardy's School for Boys.

1888   Student at the Royal Belfast Academical Institution from September 1.

1891   Completed studies November 15, 1891.

1892   Worked in the tea trade at Musgrave's Establishment, Belfast.

1904   *The Kingdom of Twilight*.

1905   Entered Christ's College, Cambridge. *The Garden God*; a short story "Pan's Pupil" in *Ulad*; "The Exhibition Pictures at the Hibernian Academy, Dublin," in *Ulad*.

1908   Was graduated from Cambridge University with second class honors in the Medieval and Modern Language Tripos. From this year until 1947, reviewed books for the *Westminster Review*, the *Northern Whig*, *Nation and Athenaeum*, *Spectator*, *Irish Statesman*, *Bookman*, and several miscellaneous periodicals to which he also contributed articles about literary figures.

1911   *The Bracknels*.

1912   *Following Darkness*.

1913   *The Gentle Lover: A Comedy of Middle Age*.

1915   *At the Door of the Gate* and *W. B. Yeats: A Critical Study*.

1916   *The Spring Song*.

1918   *A Garden By the Sea*, stories and sketches.

1919   *Pirates of the Spring*.

1922   *Pender Among the Residents*.

1926   *Apostate*; reissued without alteration in 1947. An autobiography.

1927   *Demophon: A Traveller's Tale*.

1928   *Illustrators of the Sixties*.

1929   *Walter de la Mare: A Critical Study*.

1931   *Uncle Stephen*.

1932   Elected a charter member of the Irish Academy of Letters.

1933   Awarded an Honorary Doctorate of Literature from Queen's University, Belfast.

1934 *Brian Westby*.
1936 *The Retreat; or, The Machinations of Henry*.
1937 *Peter Waring*; a revised, rewritten version of *Following Darkness*.
1940 *Private Road*; an autobiographical memoir.
1941 *Retrospective Adventures*; reprints and revisions of articles previously published.
1942 *Note and Impressions*; six essays previously printed in periodicals.
1943 *Poems from the Greek Anthology*; a translation.
1944 *Young Tom; or, Very Mixed Company*. Awarded the James Tait Black Memorial Prize for the best work of fiction published during that year.
1946 *The Milk of Paradise: Some Thoughts on Poetry*.
1947 Died January 4 at Warrenport, County Down, Northern Ireland. *Denis Bracknel*, rewritten version of *The Bracknels* published posthumously.

CHAPTER 1

A Portrait of the Artist

FORREST Reid (1875–1947), an Anglo-Irish novelist, is the " 'first Ulster writer of European status.' "[1] Edward Wagenkenecht describes him as "one of the outstanding individualists among contemporary British novelists."[2] To Russell Burlingham, whose pioneer full length study of Reid is invaluable, he is as "unusual and as idiosyncratic as his books."[3] Walter de la Mare, with whom Reid shared "half a life time 'taking in' " each other's proofs, observed that Reid, "endlessly active, . . . was yet a Dreamer; unflinchingly matter-of-fact, he had drunk the 'milk of Paradise'; and the Greek Anthology was in his bones."[4]

Historically, Forrest Reid's adult life spanned two world wars and the civil war in Ireland in 1916, the rise of totalitarianism throughout Europe, the holocaust of the Jews, the technological revolution with its so-called "theory" of progress, the disintegration of orthodox religious values, and the subsequent dehumanization of man by political systems, wars, and machines. Within these chaotic times, censorship of both press and the arts in Ireland was an existential reality. Restrictive laws denying civil rights and freedom to homosexuals were enacted in the United Kingdom and in Ireland in the aftermath of the Oscar Wilde trial; and these remained unchanged until 1967. By the Censorship Bill of 1928, no writer was free to express his views on behavior not considered "normal."[5]

The problem for Reid as a writer who had lost faith in orthodox Christianity was to find an integrating symbol for his religious beliefs and vision. The curve of his life is recorded in *Apostate* (1926) and *Private Road* (1940). *Apostate,* as a spiritual autobiography, portrays the formative years of his life to age seventeen, although it is more a self-portrait of a Romantic temperament than a series of biographical details. The title depicts "a state of mind, not a person—," that is described by its author as "the reluctance of a

15

small boy to go to church, and his 'passion for humanizing things,' his pleasure in discovering river-gods, tree-spirits, and the divinities of sun and moon."[6] Below the surface of consciousness, but always persistent, is a deep undercurrent of loneliness as the quester moves through his search for a spiritual kingdom and a Divine Friend to a realization of self-authenticity as person and writer.

Private Road, written when Reid was sixty-five, is a novelist's autobiography that records the intentions, aspirations, and public reception of his fiction. It continues the search begun in *Apostate* for a rational explanation of his religious and esthetic convictions. A portrait of the artist as an individualist, *Private Road* also contains his impressions of Cambridge University, his feeling for animals, and his recollections of friends and literary associates. Although important for the factual information it contains, *Private Road* is most significant for the light it sheds on the origin, growth, and development of Reid's creativity which has its source in dreams and in dream activity. In the final analysis, *Private Road* is a record of a pilgrim's progress toward an eternity where the ideal becomes the *"only"* real, the equivalent of the highest freedom and autonomy.

I   *Behold This Dreamer*

Born in Belfast, Ireland, on June 24, 1875, Forrest Reid was the sixth and youngest son of Robert Reid by his second wife, Frances Matilda Parr. Except for Reid's years at Cambridge University and for his occasional trips to Dublin, London, and the continent, he made his home in Belfast until his death in 1947. Outwardly, the Belfast described in Reid's *Apostate* in 1940 was considerably different from his boyhood memories of the city before the turn of the century. In the wake of the Industrial Revolution, cottages gave way to factories; businesses like Musgrave's tea warehouse, where the young Reid was later initiated into the working world at age seventeen, darkened the landscape. Below the surface, the political and religious tensions, which divided North from South, which erupted in the Easter Rebellion of 1916, and which projected to the bloody battles of the 1970's, were existential realities. Among its middle class citizens, social climbers who aped English manners and speech sent their sons to English universities.[7]

Reid's earliest recollections of Belfast and its rustic environs, as seen through the eyes of a child from Mount Charles Street, are fused with nostalgia for the Lagan River and the lake country, the

Mourne Mountains, the countryside of Donegal, Ballycastle, and the sea. Whenever the world weighed heavily upon him, or when haunting night dreams threatened him as they so often did, he escaped to the scenic suburbs and ran up Malone Road and across King's Bridge to the river. At other times, he walked across Mount Charles Street to University Place and the Linen Hall Library to lose himself in the world of romance. In those early days, he went on visits by slow train to Uncle Seaton's house at the "Glebe" in Ballinderry—visits he enjoyed more in anticipation than in realization (52–53, 139). As summer yielded to autumn, the memory of an evening at dusk in Orneau Park with a German band playing the "Lorelei" brought back memories of "the beauty of the Lagan valley, filled with the sound of hidden running water" and the beauty of the sea, "an unearthly beauty, because it washed on the shores of my dream world" (200). The sea, the river, the mountains, and the countryside are the essential geography of Reid's youth, his land of heart's desire, and the physical landscape of his novels. Although Belfast was for the most part provincial and parochial, it was in the Belfast world of high society that Reid first saw Oscar Wilde, whom his mother described as an "aesthetic, like Bunthorne in *Patience*" (54). Years later, Reid read Wilde's short stories and later still saw him sitting on a box seat beside the coachman when Wilde was a guest at College Gardens, Cambridge.

In the early chapters of *Apostate*, Reid portrays the conflict between his parents as a silent warfare about social and religious issues. "My father was a shipowner," he writes; "my mother an aristocrat" (9, 40). His father, Robert Reid, of stolid middle class stock, was descended from a long line of Presbyterian dissenters to whom Bass Rock prison symbolized persecution and exile under Charles II. He had been a shipowner in Liverpool; but, in an attempt to run the blockade during the American Civil War, he had lost his business. Subsequently, he was forced to take "a subordinate position as manager of Anderson's Felt Works" (9). Since he died when Reid was about five or six years old, he left only vague memories of the half crowns and the sovereigns that he offered his son as substitutes for affection. Deteriorating family fortunes are recorded in a succession of rented houses from the clubhouse of the Royal Ulster Yacht Club at Bangor, County Down, to 20 Mount Charles Street where Forrest was born five or six years before his father's death; and the moves ended with the house at 15 Mount Charles Street where

Reid's drama of life in two words of dream and reality began to take shape (9).

Reid's mother, descended from Katherine Parr, the last of Henry VIII's queens and a Roman Catholic, was his father's second wife. The fact that his mother's family never visited the Reid home and the knowledge that some of them were Roman Catholics fascinated Reid as a boy; he thought it very romantic to know that some of his mother's relatives "were going to hell" (40–41). Indeed, a significant aspect of Reid's early development can be seen in his relationship with and in his attitude toward his aristocratic mother. She discouraged his fondness for animals and refused to let him play with boys from other social classes until he was almost nine years old. Aloof and withdrawn, she failed to give him the warmth and love he craved as a child. She hurt him, too, by her seeming indifference and by her insensitivity to his need for affection. Although there was never any estrangement between them or any open antagonism, there appears to be a deeply rooted resentment of his mother on Reid's part. In an effort to be fair to her, he wrote that he "had a real admiration for my mother, queer and detached as the word may sound . . ." (41).

Reid's warmest memories center on his English preschool nurse, Emma Holmes, whom he immortalized in *Apostate* and in *Demophon* as Demeter, the life-giving earth mother who is gentle, affectionate, and human. Many years later a psychoanalyst told Reid that Emma was the source and well-spring of his creativity. She let him play on Sundays; she respected his rage at being confined in chapel, a feeling which Reid interprets as his "permanent reaction" to Christianity; and she gave him a sense of security, companionship, and understanding. Above all, Emma was fair; and her Christianity never interfered with his need for freedom. As she read her Wesleyan Bible on Sunday afternoons, the child at her feet built towered cities of bricks. "My cities," he writes, "were Greece, Athens and the Peloponnesian States, . . . peopled by a military crowd"; and these cities, "perpetually at war," the child as marksman shot down (21). For children growing up in Ulster then, as now, war games reveal the extent to which psychic damage occurs as religious tensions erupt into violence.[8]

After Emma's departure, Reid's recurrent dream of beauty saved the dreamer from the horror of frightening nightmares. In *Apostate*, the dream pictured an "earthly paradise" or "an enchanted land" beyond a "remote mountain" where "a bright . . . young, beautiful company" sported with "naked, unspoiled bodies" on the seashore to the "slim pipes of Pan . . . 'sad with the whole of pleasure.' " His epiphany discloses both ecstasy and fear. "It was the only heaven I wanted, or was ever to want," he exclaims. Yet the beauty of the dream garden was marred by "a crouching beast in black marble, with a panther's smooth body and a human face," which the dreamer "dared not awaken" but eventually had to reckon with (28, 76).

At age nine, in 1883, Reid attended Miss Hardy's School; here he learned mythology by rote when, in retrospect, he would have preferred the library of Apollodorus (121). From 1888–1891, he attended the Royal Academical Institution, which publicly followed a traditional Classical curriculum.[9] Privately, he discovered a world of romance, philosophy, and the Classics in the Linen Hall Library. In the poetry of Edgar Allen Poe's "Ulalume," "The Raven," and the "Sleeper," he found the atmosphere of his dream world; in Victor Hugo's romances, the mind behind the work; in Helen Mather's *Coming Through the Rye*, a tragic ending; and, in each of Rhoda Broughton's novels, a tragic climax in a passionate vision. The youth described in *Apostate* preferred the imaginative intensity of these works to *Daily Light*, the spiritual reading formerly thrust upon him (128, 186). Robert Lynd, his classmate, remembers him as a loner and as "a solitary engrossed in his own thoughts and indifferent to the world immediately around him."[10] After graduation from high school, Reid suffered severe states of loneliness, depression, and feelings of alienation that culminated in a half-hearted attempt at suicide by taking laudanum. As Reid watches over the shoulder of the boy he was at sixteen, this attempt at self-annihilation seems to have been an unconscious wish to obliterate a world in which an adolescent's difference and precocity had no place.

From a child's refusal to attend church services to the adolescent's rejection of a formal, creedal religion is a short but logical step. Autobiographically, *Apostate* serves as Reid's explanation of his discovery of the Greek world of values through reading and personal experience—a discovery that was simultaneous with his rejection of formal Christianity. Reid's apostasy, as he remembered it, occurred on the very day of his confirmation at St. Thomas' Church, Belfast; but his rejection was only the visible sign of an already existent invisible state: "Its beginnings were bound up with the first dream I ever dreamed. . . . . It was not . . . so much that I disbelieved in the Christian creed (though I did now disbelieve in it) as that temperamentally I was antagonistic to this religion, to its doctrines, its theory of life, the shadow it cast across the earth" (204). The steps in the process of rejection were adequately set by the young Reid's questioning of the varieties of Christian religious denominations and by experiences he had encountered along the way. First he rejects the hell-haunted carnality with which the Reverend Mr. Farrington is obsessed and then the evangelism of Miss Crouch with her sentimental questions of "one's relations to Jesus" (128–32). This early rejection of Christianity, with its subsequent feeling of freedom from a guilt-ridden Protestant ethic, liberated him to discover not only his own authenticity but also an esthetic within which to structure a value system more congenial to his temperament.

Parallel passages from childhood and adolescence sound the note of apostasy and discovery. As a child, his rebellion centered on compulsory church attendance, which this passionate outburst reveals: "I hated Sunday, I hated church, I hated Sunday school, I hated Bible stories. I hated everybody mentioned in both the Old and New Testaments, except perhaps the impenitent thief, Eve's snake, and a few similar characters"(19). After his rejection of the Church of Ireland (Anglican), animism answers his need for a spirit that gives unity to life: "If only I had been asked to worship and to love the earth I could have done it so easily! If only the earth had been God. The tender green on the trees, the mossy lawns, the yellow daffodils—all these were lovely, and Sunday made no difference to them. Everything seemed to live a natural life on Sundays except people. Cows, birds, cats, dogs, all lived exactly as cows, birds, cats, and dogs had lived from the beginning of the world" (19, 148). When animism replaced his Christocentric religion, Reid chose the Humanism of Socrates for his ethical imperative.

The intermediate stage in the process of childhood maturation, which involves personal relationships to peers and friends, was, for an older Reid looking back on his youth, a strange yet wonderful period. The point at which a boy is aware of other boys before awakening to girls and sex is sensitively portrayed through the use of three separate adventures, each complete in itself although it contains a core of meaning later utilized in his later novels. The first experience depicts his visit to the room of an English schoolboy philatelist, ostensibly for the purpose of comparing hobbies; but the visit becomes in reality Reid's first introduction to overtures that he rejected. In the second incident, the young Reid becomes an unwilling accomplice to an older boy, Alan Cunningham, in the act of breaking into and entering an unoccupied house. This nocturnal adventure, begun as a dream of perfect friendship, ended in disappointment and in disillusionment. At the age of sixteen, when he was awakening to sex, he visited the house of a woman known for her sexual promiscuity. Unlike Jerome's reaction in André Gide's *Strait is the Gate*, Reid's response, as he relates it, was both natural and guilt free.

II *Friendship and Seed Time*

Because Reid's financial condition precluded a university education, he became a tea trade apprentice in Musgrave's establishment; but he would have preferred a position in the Print Room of the British Museum. Musgrave's became, however, a vital experience, because he met James Quigley and Andrew Rutherford, who not only made his adjustment possible but also had a formative effect on his life. Quigley, the archetypal wise man, brought the pastoral world of Homer and Theocritus to life by his gift for storytelling. He was "a pagan who had never heard of paganism: his mind was simple and earthy, unspiritual and entirely free from corruption" (226). Long before this friendship, Reid had arrived at the Greek view of nature by reading the poems of Sappho and Theocritus, and lyrical passages from the Greek dramatists where he found spiritual kinship:

. . . in wood and river and plant and animal and bird and insect it had seemed to me there was a spirit which was the same as my spirit. And here, in this poetry, every aspect of nature seemed to be perpetually passing into divinity, into the forms and radiance of a god, while the human passed no less easily into tree or reed or flower. Adonis, Narcissus, Syrinx, Daphne—could I not see them with my own eyes? Could I not see Philomela flying low above the earth? Had I not, even in this land once blessed by Saint Patrick, caught a glimpse of that ill-mannered boy who, mocking the great Demeter while she drank, was straightway transformed into a lizard? The landscape was the landscape I loved best, a landscape proclaiming the vicinity of man, a landscape imbued with a human spirit that was yet somehow divine. (207)

In the Homeric hymns, he also found an animistic response to nature, wherein the life force thrusts against death in cyclic time:

"At the birth of the nymphs," I read in the *Hymn to Aphrodite*, "there sprang up pine-trees or tall-crested oaks on the fruitful earth, flourishing and fair. . . . But when the fate of death approaches, first do the trees wither on the ground, and the bark about them moulders, and the twigs fall down, and even as the trees perish so the soul of the nymph leaves the light of the sun." It was a world in which either everything was spirit or nothing was: and it was young, there was a freshness even in the hottest sunshine. (207–208)

Although Greek religion, cults, and myths colored Reid's imagination, they did not awaken his faith. His deities were Pan and Hermes, the lesser Arcadian gods portrayed by poets and sculptors; to Reid, Pan and Hermes, "deities I invoked or evoked, were friendly, and more than half human." The darker, mystical element "interwoven with the worship of Dionysius (the *truly* religious element, . . . with its blood-sacrifices and ecstasy, and mingled lust and madness) . . . was repellent to me because of the cruelty bound up with it" (210–11). From his reading in Platonic philosophy, he discovered the wisdom of Socrates as a confirmation of the thoughts, emotions, and dreams that had haunted him from childhood. "It was a paganism softened, orientalized . . . to bring it into accord with what I desired; nevertheless, what appealed to me *was* to be found in the literature of Greece, and not elsewhere." In his study, Reid hung a print of Socrates and another of Hermes of Praxiteles as his guardians both human and divine (205–206).

Sixteen years later, when writing *Private Road*, he returned to this earlier epiphany as he placed his discovery of his latent homosexuality on the line in order to dispel once and for all any doubts that his readers might have about his individualism: "I could imagine nobody wiser or better than Socrates . . . he belonged to, was in my world. All the dangers that encompassed me were dangers he himself had felt and understood and conquered." In the traditional Socrates, surrounded by "a ring of embryo philosophers," Reid found a vital mentor, one who never lost touch with humanity even when contemplating eternity (90–92).

The value of friendship as an ideal relationship that Reid discovered in Socrates also governed his friendship with Andrew Rutherford, a fellow apprentice, who seemed the embodiment of the radiant half of his dream. The friendship shared with Andrew was deep, "the deeper for being unexpressed"; and it lasted throughout

Reid's life (PR,11). In *Apostate*, Reid explains that life in the old warehouse took on a different dimension: it became a wonderful "voyage of discovery to be undertaken no longer alone" (232). Together, the friends explored a world of books and ideas. Reid interested Rutherford in poetry; Rutherford tried to interest him in astronomy, geology, and physics. When the Rutherford family, who were deeply religious, discovered that Edward Caird's *Evolution of Religion* and Herbert Spencer's *First Principles* were also shared reading, they made their displeasure known. Moreover, when Reid let Andrew read his private journal, which recorded his innermost thoughts, he suddenly observed the disappointment that was evident in his friend's silence upon closing the book.

Reid's friendship with Rutherford was the means by which he broke through to both art and life. If we are to understand Reid's unique qualities as a writer, his search for a companion in youth becomes a writer's search for intellectual and spiritual compatibility based on a common vision of life; and such a vision was later realized in Walter de la Mare in whom he found a kindred spirit. Symbolically, for both Reid and William Hale White, who wrote under the pseudonym of Mark Rutherford, the search for a friend became a religious quest for permanence and spiritual values. In his *Autobiography* Rutherford wrote:

> I always felt . . . that talk with whom I would, I left something unsaid which was precisely what I most wished to say. I wanted a friend who would sacrifice himself to me utterly, and to whom I might offer a similar sacrifice. I found companions for whom I cared, and who professed to care for me; but I was thirsting for deeper draughts of love than any which they had to offer; and I said to myself that if I were to die, not one of them would remember me for more than a week. This was not selfishness, for I longed to prove my devotion as well as to receive that of another. How this ideal haunted me! It made me restless and anxious at the sight of every new face, wondering whether at last I had found that for which I searched as if for the kingdom of heaven. It is superfluous to say that a friend of the kind I wanted never appeared.[11]

If a friend could not understand the interiority of Reid's conflict, then the anonymous reader who does understand becomes the perfect friend who shares the journey to awareness. Each of Reid's works is confessional to a greater or lesser degree, but his writing also reveals a quality of mind that is reflected in a quality of style.

III *Cambridge Memories*

Between 1891 and Reid's entrance to Cambridge University in 1905, he wrote two novels, *The Kingdom of Twilight* and *The Garden God*. In each narrative, Reid treats of a precocious boy's relationship to his peers, to his school, and to the process of maturation. Publication of an earlier novel, originally entitled *The River* (the Lagan), was delayed until 1905 because of the proximity of Eden Phillpot's novel, *The River*. In 1904, with the publication of *The Kingdom of Twilight*, Reid's public career as a novelist began. The subject portrayed in it of a sensitive, imaginative boy's response to the world continued to be his preoccupation for forty-three years. Reid well knew the limits of his range, which he described in *Private Road* as Mr. Dick's "obsession with King Charles' Head" (14); and by use of this plurisignificant image, he linked his preoccupation with the world as seen through the eyes of an exceptional boy to Charles Dickens' treatment of eccentricity and to the long line of Irish-Presbyterian dissenters and nonconformists against the Anglican establishment. The local historical setting of Belfast and its environs, its topography and its sense of the place, provided a rich mine of material from which he drew his inspiration. By contrasting city and country, he creates a pattern of time and timelessness, of time past and time present as they interlock, overlap, merge, and flow into the ocean of the future. From the perspective of two worlds in collision, seen through the eyes of a growing boy's consciousness of change, Reid portrays a search for permanence and for Humanistic values.

In 1904, Reid also learned about the Ulster Renaissance, a movement designed to encourage young writers of promise to accomplish for Northern Ireland what was already being done successfully by the Irish Literary Renaissance in Dublin. At the invitation of W. B. Reynolds, Reid was asked to contribute the article "The Future of Irish Opera" to the literary organ *Ulad*, a periodical modeled on William Butler Yeats's *Samhain* (PR, 36). Since Reid recognized the movement as propaganda against the South, knew of no such thing as "Ulster genius," or saw any future in Irish opera, he declined the dubious honor of being a music critic. Subsequently, he contributed to the three editions of *Ulad* two articles and the short story "Pan's Pupil," a story that locates the source of Reid's creativity in Greek mythology and in modern Belfast.

Upon the death of his mother, a small inheritance enabled Reid to consider a university education. Encouraged and tutored by James Rutherford, who later took orders in the Presbyterian Church, Reid passed the entrance examinations for Christ's College, Cambridge, although William Paley's *Evidences of Christianity* was still a requirement for admission as a testament of belief. He attended Christ's College from October, 1905, to June, 1908, when he was graduated with a Bachelor of Arts degree and second class honors in the Modern and Medieval Languages Tripos.[12] In *Private Road* he writes that, from an educational point of view, Cambridge failed to live up to his expectations. At age thirty, with an established view of life already formed and with a writer's love of language and literature, he found "an almost total absence of any genuine interest in literature either early or contemporary" (PR, 54). English and French were "objects" of study rather than vital disciplines, although in his estimation Classical literature was treated with more sensitivity. Anglo-Saxon, taught by W. W. Skeat, the eminent philologist, was a vital learning experience. The portrait of Skeat, as he traced on the blackboard the origin of a word "with specimens from every language ever spoken," later became Professor Heron in Reid's *Pender Among the Residents* (PR, 59–60).

Skeat's passion for words, like Professor G. C. Macaulay's love of Shakespeare, contrasted sharply with the lectures of Professor Israel Gollancz in Middle English which, though "lively and punctuated with jokes," failed to touch the depths of literature. Although Reid gave a copy of his second novel *The Garden God* to Gollancz, the professor never acknowledged receipt of the book; and from his constrained manner at their next meeting, Reid knew that the eminent professor had disapproved. Reid thought, however, that apparently it was too much to expect specialists in Medieval and Renaissance literature to have a feeling for contemporary writing: "Literature belonged to the past; and its exponents approached it as one might the stuffed birds and beasts in a museum" (PR, 59).

Student life at Cambridge, as Reid recalls it in *Private Road*, also contrasts sharply with the accounts of the Apostles Club described by John Maynard Keynes and Leonard Woolf. Reid's recollection of a dinner in Ronald Firbank's rooms at King's College in an atmosphere of "drugged cigarettes," orchids, and evening dress seemed as unreal as Firbank himself; for Reid describes him as a "decadent of the school of Oscar Wilde, but lacking Wilde's intellect." Reid was amused by Firbank's habit of name dropping to associate himself with celebrities such as M. de Max, Catulles Mendès, Pierre

Louÿs, and Alfred Douglas. Unlike E. M. Forster, who thought
Firbank a minor genius, Reid believed him to be genuine after his
fashion—that of imitating and hovering between Wilde and Norman
Douglas. Rupert Brooke, however, is more sympathetically mentioned as showing literary promise (PR, 58, 55).

Because of Reid's interest in contemporary literature, he joined
the Irish Society at Cambridge. When he read a paper on Yeats,
which became the core of his work *W. B. Yeats: A Critical Study*
(1915), he discovered that no one in the society had ever heard of
Yeats! His association with the Mermaid Society, composed of students in the literary tripos, was likewise a short-lived one since the
approach to literature in both groups was utilitarian, whereas Reid's
was appreciative. His feeling for rhythm in music and in literature,
like that of Padraic Colum, was part of their Irish inheritance.

During college holidays Reid traveled to museums and galleries
in London, Belgium, and Switzerland; and he made notes about his
impressions of paintings which much later became the substance of
two critical works: *Retrospective Adventures* (1941) and *Notes and
Impressions* (1942). Following his Cambridge days, he began a conscious search for spiritual values; and three letters inserted into the
text of *Private Road* record his correspondence with persons whose
lives revealed a struggle with religious problems. In comparative
religions he hoped to find a unifying principle and a way of life such
as "A. E." (George Russell) had found in Oriental mysticism or to
discover at least a meaning comparable to what Andrew Rutherford
had found in the Gospels after he had abandoned formal Christianity. For this purpose, Reid went to Dublin to visit "A. E." at his
home (PR, 126), where their conversation at first centered on a
discussion of psychical experiences, symbolism, telepathy, and the
experiments of the Society for Psychical Research. When "A. E."
counseled Reid to concentrate on a triangle to approach the mystic
way, however, Reid terminated his visit because "the Eastern mysticism of 'A.' E. was as alien from my way of thinking as was Christianity. . . . It did not attract me; I did not like it; I was outside the
pale. . . . A pagan I went to 'A. E.' and a pagan, . . . at heart and in
spirit, I bade farewell to him" (PR, 133, 141).

IV   *Conscience and Censorship*

With the publication of *The Garden God: A Tale of Two Boys*
(1905), which treats the friendship theme, Reid experienced one of

the first setbacks in his literary career. Although Henry James encouraged Reid during the composition of *The Kingdom of Twilight*, he refused to accept the dedication of *The Garden God*. Moreover, the unnecessary furor caused by both the public and professional criticism of this book was another disappointment. In *Private Road*, Reid asked: "Why," should what "had been academically acceptable for over two thousand years suddenly cease to be acceptable because I had translated it out of the world of dialectic into that of fiction? I had not altered it. It had been formulated by Socrates as an ideal, and as an ideal I had kept it." Reid's question was reasonable enough, since Howard Sturgis' *Tim*, published fourteen years earlier, had been one of the most successful novels of its year, although it was not Reid's kind of book (PR, 66, 65).

Russell Burlingham explains that the social shibboleths of the era, coupled with the proximity of the Wilde scandal and the repugnancy of the public toward any form of unusual emotional relationship, were the factors that accounted for Henry James's response to *The Garden God*.[13] The sympathy of Edmund Gosse was far more generous; for, in an undated letter from Regent's Park that was reprinted in *Private Road*, Gosse stated his belief in the importance of freedom for the individual and the writer "to be a law unto himself" as long as it in no way interfered with the rights of others. Reid doubtless took comfort from Gosse's advice as he had from the earlier advice of André Raffalovitch, who had urged him not to accept defeat and to write a story about the youth of William Beckford (PR, 72, 81). Although Reid believed that Beckford's life contained a story, considerable spadework would be necessary and so he did not write it. Since his interest lay in the exceptional youth, he contemplated writing a life of the child prodigy, Wolfgang Mozart, a life of Thomas Chatterton, or an imaginative life of Christ; but he finally abandoned these subjects as "false starts." Consciously, he placed himself in the tradition of individualists from Socrates to André Gide whose personal convictions gave testimony to the long struggle of conscience against censorship. It is interesting to note that E. M. Forster's novel *Maurice*, written between 1913 and 1915, was withheld from publication at the author's request until after his death.[14]

During the composition of *The Bracknels: A Family Chronicle* (1911), Reid lived with the Reverend James Rutherford, assistant to the Reverend Dr. Workman, in the Presbyterian rectory at South-

parade in Belfast. In this novel, when Reid treated the theme of a
boy's awakening to friendship within a Realistic framework, the
reading public accepted it with little protest. While wrestling with a
method for *Following Darkness* (1912), rewritten as *Peter Waring*
(1937), Reid became convinced that the years of childhood, boyhood, and adolescence were the most significant stages for his vision
as well as for the limits of his sympathy. At this time he met Walter
de la Mare and E. M. Forster, whose friendships and literary associations lasted throughout his life. Moreover, Reid's *Walter de la
Mare: A Critical Study* (1929) is a perceptive study of the writer as a
visionary.

In a detailed letter to Reid from Basil de Selincourt dated 1914,
the subject of the relationship between psychic experience and
spiritual vision is probed. As this letter appears in *Private Road*, it is
an answer to Reid's search for a rational explanation of spiritual and
psychic phenomena (PR, 169–79). By 1915, Reid arrived at the
belief that art was "coming to take the place of religion, or itself
becomes a kind of religion in being the medium by which we pass
from the material to the spiritual world. . . . The artist, therefore,
will do well to return to a spirit of the past when men worshipped
nature. . . ."[15]

V   *Hermes and Socrates*

From 1912 to 1922, beginning with *Following Darkness* (1912),
The Gentle Lover (1913), *At the Door of the Gate* (1915), *Spring
Song* (1916), *Pirates of the Spring* (1919), and *Pender Among the
Residents* (1922), Reid continued to explore unusual states of mind
and feeling in children and in adolescents as their values conflict
with those of adults with limited vision. Meanwhile, he wrote book
reviews for the *Manchester Guardian* and the *Irish Statesman* under
the editorship of "A. E." until the Censorship Bill brought about the
demise of the *Irish Statesman* in 1930. He also published *A Garden
by the Sea: A Collection of Short Stories and Sketches* (1918), a
tribute to the spirit of youth, whose vision he celebrated in each
successive work. In 1928, his hobby of collecting prints became a
scholarly volume of art criticism, *Illustrators of the Sixties*. This
classic work about Victorian English woodcut artists includes selections from Arthur Hughes, Dante Gabriel Rossetti, John Dawson
Watson, and others not elsewhere studied at such length nor with
such originality.

Following the publication of *Apostate* in 1926, Reid wrote *Demophon: A Traveller's Tale* (1927), making Demophon the correlative of the boy in *Apostate;* Demeter, his childhood nurse, Emma; and Hermes, the dream playmate. While writing *Demophon,* Reid became persuaded that "some intelligence" outside his own "was imposing itself" on him. He wondered if this spirit could have originated "in some universal spiritual force from which Christianity and all religions had sprung" (PR, 199). In search of an authorative account of the possible existence of a Hermes cult in comparative religious symbolism, he wrote to André Raffalovitch, a Russian of Jewish origin who had converted to Roman Catholicism. In reply, Raffalovitch enclosed a quotation from an "authority" without naming his source. In *Private Road,* Reid commented with considerable irony on "the verdict of the Catholic Church" as transcribed by Raffalovitch (PR, 200). Granting the possibility that the ideal that Raffalovitch had found in Christ might be the analogue of Reid's Hermes, the unnamed counsellor wrote:

Your friend can find in his Hermes whatever spirit he likes to evolve out of his hungers and desires, and this ideal of his (in so far as it consorts with the ideals painted for us in the New Testament) is no doubt the same spiritual ideal as you have found in Christ, or rather one facet of it. Unhappily I know nothing of his Hermes, so that I don't know what his ideals signify: but it is clear that Christ is the fulfilment of all our earlier hopes and the reality of our later dreams, so that there, in Christ, all religions touch hands. But it is only His own revelation to us of Himself and of God that gives us *fully* the meaning and reality of our hopes and hungers. Yet though His revelation is as complete as can be, our apprehension of it is not complete. We see darkly, and that in a mirror. (PR, 200)

From the tone of this letter, Reid gathered that, unless he abandoned Hermes and accepted the institutional church, he would forever remain outside the pale. Since the spirit Reid sought was inextricably rooted in nature, he sought "a god, but not God, not the creator and controller of the universe" (PR, 201). The position of Raffalovitch's counsellor was as unsatisfactory as the opinion of François Mauriac, who wrote to Reid that " 'Christ enlighteneth every man that cometh into the world' " (PR, 201). Neither position enlightened Reid, since it did not include him. "As I have said," he wrote, "I believe, with Socrates, that we can only really love what is good, but it would be as idle to pretend that the spirit hovering

before my imagination in the least resembled Christ, as to affirm
that among our earthly friends we must all feel drawn towards and
love the same person" (PR, 201). For Reid, the good that he loves,
"translated into Christian mythology" is "much more like the angel
who accompanies the youthful Tobias on his adventures" (PR, 201).

VI   *Golden Days in Ulster*

Under the influence of Walter de la Mare, Reid's next three
novels, *Uncle Stephen* (1931), *Brian Westby* (1934), and *The Retreat;
or, The Machinations of Henry* (1936), treat the problems of an
exceptionally imaginative boy in his relationship to family, peers,
friends, and time. Four years after *The Retreat*, Reid published his
second autobiography, *Private Road* (1940). The following year he
collected the best of his critical essays on books and writers, as well
as miscellaneous essays and tales, which were published as *Retrospective Adventures* (1941). Master Romney Robinson, Emily
Brontë, Henry James, W. H. Hudson, Arthur Rimbaud, Richard
Garnett, Arthur Lyon Raile, and Seumas O'Kelley, among others,
come to life in these pages. The sense of the place in "Bruges" is
impressionistically recreated. In the portrait "Kenneth," and in the
tales "Courage," "The White Kitten," and "An Ulster Farm,"
memories of a happy past in Northern Ireland emerge. In 1943,
Poems from the Greek Anthology appeared as a testament to Reid's
appreciation for Greek love poetry. In his final novel, *Young Tom;
or, Very Mixed Company* (1944), he surpasses each of his previous
works in brilliance and sincerity. With the publication of *The Milk
of Paradise: Some Thoughts on Poetry* (1946), a perceptive, critical
study of imaginative writers including Coleridge and Poe, Reid
closed a lifetime of creativity.

Like Henry James, Reid's literary mentor and idol, his life was
devoted to writing novels, book reviews, and criticism that earned
him a reputation in literary circles. For many years before his death
in 1947, he lived in a small house in Ormiston Crescent on the
outskirts of his beloved Belfast, rooted in the legendary past but
always in close touch with the present. Except for Reid's occasional
journeys to London to see the opera, of which he was a devotee, or
to visit his friend and literary adviser, Walter de la Mare, he spent
most of his days in Belfast surrounded by his books, his writing, and
his friends. His circle of friends included Andrew and James Rutherford, Walter de la Mare, E. M. Forster, John Gilbert, S. Knox

Cunningham, J. N. Hart, George Buchanan, J. N. Bryson, Mrs. Workman, Arthur Greeves, Robin Perry, and Stephen Gilbert, his literary executor, whose first novel, *The Landslide,* is dedicated to Reid.[16] Mr. Gilbert skillfully captures the familiar image of the ageless Reid in the following vignette:

People who lived near him knew that he was an author, but most of them had not read his books. They regarded a man who did not go into business every day as something of a phenomenon; they laughed when he played cricket on the street with their children, but they liked him, and knowing the difficulties of a solitary bachelor, some of them—particularly Mr. Harvey and Mrs. Crawford—helped him in many small matters. The children liked him even more. He played games with them as one of themselves. More than once, arriving in Ormiston Crescent to go for a walk with him, I have found him in the middle of a hot argument as to whose turn it was to bat next—the wicket was usually the lamp-post outside his gate. I felt a hundred years older at nineteen.[17]

During his final years, Reid lived an active life that included writing and collecting books and being honored. His love of imaginative literature is reflected in his large collection of Greek and French classics; his collection of the works of Henry James that included several early, unpublished stories; and his first editions of many writers, such as William Butler Yeats and Walter de la Mare. He also collected puzzles, stamps, wallpapers, and butterflies.[18] In 1932 Reid was elected a charter member of the Irish Academy of Letters;[19] in 1933, he was awarded an honorary doctorate of literature from Queen's University, Belfast;[20] and in 1944, his novel, *Young Tom,* was awarded the James Tait Black Memorial Prize for the best work of fiction published during that year.[21] After Forrest Reid died, in Warrenport, Northern Ireland, on January 6, 1947, the Forrest Reid Memorial Prize was inaugurated in his memory at the Royal Belfast Academical Institution "for the best short story or poem submitted by the boys of the school" in any given year.[22]

His classmate, Robert Lynd, remembered Reid as an "enthusiastic lover of Plato and Anatole France, and [as] a collector of every scrap that Henry James had ever written."[23] Of his sincerity and integrity, Stephen Gilbert wrote: "He had the most utter contempt for people who compromised with their consciences." Of his stature as a writer, he says: "In my opinion he was the only Ulsterman who ever made a considerable contribution to British Literature."[24]

CHAPTER 2

The Literary Milieu

W HEN *The Bookman* of London sponsored a symposium on "The Artist and the World Today," Reid was one of several writers to define the relationship of their works to the conditions of modern times. When asked, "Can you as an artist disregard the state of things?" Reid replied: "In the sense that the question is meant—Yes. 'La littérature n'a et ne peut avoir d'objet que le beau.' But that leaves it less open to the artist to express his views of an explicitly didactic or critical nature." To his next question, "How can you define the relevance of your art to existing conditions?", he responded: "It has no more and no less relevance to them than the Odyssey has to 'existing conditions' of the age of Homer, or than 'A Mid-Summer Night's Dream' has to those of the Elizabethan Age."[1]

Reid never changed his conviction that the spiritual world offers far more opportunity for conscious artistry than the world of everyday reality. Just as the beautiful did not preclude the ugly—or the good, the evil—the dimension of the "other" was too important to sacrifice on the altar of relevance in its limited sense. Since Reid did not belong to a literary circle or to a clique; and since, as E. M. Forster says, he did not "know how to pull wires or to advertise himself,"[2] it is difficult to place him in a fixed literary or intellectual category. His individual talent and genius can be measured by placing him in time, in order to show his relationship to his own contemporaries, to the Hellenic tradition which he uses so capably, and to modern writers whose fiction reveals a comparable concern for Humanistic values.

I *Apostate in Exile*

In the tradition of the modern novel of imaginative Realism from 1890 to World War II and the present, Reid's major novels from *Uncle Stephen* to *Young Tom* may be compared with the early minor fiction of Joseph Conrad, Henry James, Ivan Turgenev, Thomas Mann, Herman Melville, and Herman Hesse. Among Anglo-Irish novelists, he resembles Joseph Sheridan Le Fanu and Wilkie Collins in their use of the supernatural. In the tradition of the English novel, he shares a spiritual vision of life with Emily Brontë, Walter de la Mare, Virginia Woolf, and J. R. R. Tolkien. With autobiographical novelists about adolescence,[3] he kept illustrious company, since his *Following Darkness* (1912) preceded Compton Mackenzie's *Sinister Street* (1913) by one year and James Joyce's *A Portrait of the Artist as a Young Man* (1916) by four years.

Among neo-Georgians in the modern story of terror, Reid resembles Robert Louis Stevenson,[4] Arthur Machen,[5] and E. M. Forster.[6] Reid also has been compared with Alain-Fournier and Marcel Proust in their common use of "recollections of things past" as comment about present discontent.[7] His similarity to the Russian novelist Ivan Aksakoff, to André Gide,[8] to Charles Dickens, and to Edmund Gosse has also been noted.[9] In his passionate individualism he may be likened to Olive Schreiner, W. H. Hudson, and Stella Benson. Although Reid began by imitating the fin de siècle style of Walter Pater and Gabriel D'Annunzio, he perfected his art by studying Henry James's technique and the "Greek ideal" of Anatole France's style.

Like other modern writers whose works span two wars, Reid's voice is raised against wars that "politicians . . . seem unable to avoid";[10] wars in which the youth of each country is sacrificed daily in the clash of ideologies for world domination. Each of his works is a tribute to youths who deserve a better world. "In Memoriam," a poem about S. J. Ireland, who was in the King's Liverpool Regiment and who was "killed in action, 12th October, 1916," is used by Reid not only to introduce his volume *Retrospective Adventures* but also to express his lament for one lost life—a lament that functions for legions who fall in war's wake:

> . . . Have you taken with you dream and poetry—
> That none will ever write, since it was yours—
> Taken them down into that world of darkness
> Where you lie now so quietly, at rest and alone?
> ....
> All that you had you gave—your life, your youth,
> Your youth's ambition—gave all ungrudgingly.

> They have taken all, and left you dead, and heedless
> Of what may be. . . .[11]

In World War II, when air raid shelters became a necessary precaution against the German blitzkrieg, Reid submitted reluctantly to the long arm of Hitler's tyranny against persons and peaceful occupations. He regarded mechanized warfare as the ultimate symbol of the technological revolution that was daily dehumanizing man; that interfered with the good life; that destroyed nature's harmony; that perpetuated the forces of darkness. For other mechanized intrusions on privacy between the years 1880–1916, he asserted that he would "sweep away . . . motor cars, aeroplanes, wireless, movies, talkies, and gramophones," because they were limitations on an individual's enjoyment of a more quiet world.[12]

From World War I to his death, Reid belonged with the resurgence of novelists who used fantasy as the means to establish their values. In times of crisis, such writers represent "the march of the human spirit" in its attempt to survive in a world of crumbling values. Through fantasy, Reid was able to say "something about life which could not be said within the naturalistic frame of reference"; and he appealed to an audience capable of realizing that "the countries of the mind are real countries, legitimate to build, legitimate to inhabit."[13] With Naturalists or with Realists like William Makepeace Thackeray and Jane Austen, whose works seem to acquiesce "in the world and in life as it is," he had nothing in common. As a Romanticist whose vision of life was colored by Hellenism, he believed that "the primary impulse of the artist springs from discontent, and his art is a crying for Elysium."[14] Beneath the surface of great art is a "divine homesickness, that same longing for an Eden from which each one of us is exiled." "For me," Reid admitted, "it may be in the Islands of the Blest . . . for you the jewelled splendor of the New Jerusalem. Only in no case, I think, is it our own free creation. It is a country whose image was stamped upon our soul before we opened our eyes on earth, and all our life is little more than a trying to get back there, our art than a mapping of its mountains and streams."[15]

To the modern novel, Reid brought a Celtic racial inheritance and temperament as the basis of his Romanticism. He has a Celt's feeling for mystery, the remote, and the distant; for the supernatural in the natural; for psychic states of feeling; and, of course, for dreams.

Even his nostalgic longing for Greece as his imaginary kingdom is a conscious writer's choice that may be considered congruent with a Celtic longing "for a great invisible past of impossible magnificence."[16] The Celtic realization of the unseen world near at hand and the Greek belief in inevitable Fate are fused in Reid's particular genius.

Although his feeling for Northern Ireland is deep, it is not partisan. In describing "A. E.", who personified the best qualities of North and South, as "a symbol of a United Ireland," Reid voiced his hope for the reconciliation of "opposites."[17] The effect of both clerical and public censorship of John Millington Synge's *Playboy of the Western World* and on Yeats's *The Countess of Kathleen* also conditioned Reid's literary reviews for the *Irish Statesman*, which was edited by "A. E." When Reid submitted an article entitled "Bishops and Black Magic," a review of Richard Garnett's *Twilight of the Gods*, "A. E." wrote by return post: "*In the name of God* find another title! . . . You can guess what your article associating Bishops with Black Magic would lead to. . . ."[18] Despite the efforts of "A. E.," Yeats, and Padraic Colum to prevent it, the Censorship Bill was passed in 1928.[19]

Reid's belief that significant knowledge comes through feeling rather than through reason was inherited from the Romantic tradition of English poets to whom he owed so much. William Wordsworth's animism, Percy Bysshe Shelley's revolutionary Idealism, John Keats's Hellenism, William Blake's Neoplatonism, and Samuel Taylor Coleridge's Transcendentalism may be seen by the perceptive reader as individual strands in the fabric of Reid's "felt thought." In the Victorian conflict between Hebraism and Hellenism, Reid chose the Greek way rather than Hebraism or Christianity as his guide to the spiritual life. His quarrel with creedal Christianity and with Christ reveals considerable antagonism if not hostility. He rejects institutional Christianity "for the shadow it cast upon the earth,"[20] and Christ, on whose birth, death, and resurrection Christianity is predicated. He also rejects the Judaic tradition because, like Christianity, it seemed to allow no place for nonconformists. Like Matthew Arnold and William Butler Yeats, he believed that art would replace religion as the means by which a spiritual revolution would occur.[21] Like Walter Pater, Reid's faith was built upon compassion, which is the ethical basis of his Humanism.

In the various societies that historically developed with the de-
cline of institutional religion and religious authority, Reid had little
interest. For the Society for Psychical Research under Madame
Blavatsky, the Society of the Golden Dawn, the Rosicrucian Society, the Fabian and other Utopian societies, he shows only nominal
concern. Although not unkind to the endeavors of these groups, he
shows them in the context of his novels as inadequate in bringing
man into communion with nature. In the final pages of *Private
Road*, however, he describes a dream (set in a Greek temple) in
which a young boy is initiated into the mysteries of a religion similar in its ancient rites to the Eleusinian mysteries and to
Freemasonry.[22] From Reid, the boy who created "an imaginary
Greece" on the banks of his native river, to Reid, the man whose
imagination is mythopoeic, Greece is the source of his inspiration
and the answer to his search for a more durable scheme of values.
Although Reid is a product of his age in many ways, he is also a
symbol of the artist against society. Because he "excluded from his
world what he considered irrelevant to his purposes he was . . . a
very subjective writer, and in the depth of his subjectivity lay the
source of his strength."[23]

II *Romantic Hellenism*

For a writer whose approach to reality is Romantic, Hellenism is
"a sentimental admiration and idealization of Greek antiquity"[24]
that is different from the pure Hellenism of native Greek writers. To
the Romantic Hellenist, Greece is a symbol of perfection in art and
life. The pastoral Arcadian world of timelessness is the analogue for
primitive, simple, natural existence that thrusts against the tensions
and violence of modern life. In Classical sculpture and poetry, ideal
beauty is humanized to give dignity and meaning to life; and the
result is unlike that of modern Realism or Naturalism, which portray
man's limitations.

From his *The Kingdom of Twilight* through his *Young Tom* to his
translations for his *Poems from the Greek Anthology*, published
shortly before his death in 1947, the Hellenic tradition shaped
Reid's thinking about religion, philosophy, ethics, art, and life; but
his personal esthetic aims were integrated in an intellectual and
artistic personality. He had an excellent command of Classical
Greek; he read and collected works of French and German Hellenists; and he inherited the Hellenic tradition from the English

Romantic, Victorian, and modern writers who kept this tradition alive.[25] His acknowledged sources of Hellenism include Homer, Theocritus, the Greek dramatists, *The Greek Anthology*, and the *Dialogues* of Plato.[26] Among modern continental Hellenists, Reid cited Anatole France as his master in directing him toward the Greek ideal; for he had found that "the charm, the natural grace, the simplicity and lucidity of France's style created a new ideal, or revived an old one, a return to the Greek spirit." As a qualification, he added: "I could not imitate that style, but somehow it set me free to discover my own."[27]

When George Seferis compares Constantin Cavafy and T. S. Eliot on the uses of the past, he laments that "classical Greece, Byzantine Greece and modern Greece are disconnected and independent countries" that modern writers and scholars chose according to their areas of specialization instead of seeing Greece as a 'whole' whose "living art . . . is part of a living tradition."[28] This statement, however, is more applicable to Eliot than to Reid. It is precisely the "living tradition" of Greece, though rooted in Classical antiquity, that Reid uses as the symbol of his mythical kingdom to order his peaceful vision of life. Although it is not possible to develop in detail here the extent to which the politico-religious problems of ancient Greece and modern Ireland are a struggle for freedom against complex forces of oppression, the appeal of Greek ideals, especially the *Antigone* of Sophocles, to the nonviolent civil rights workers in Belfast and in Derry lives on in the annals of recent history. Stephen Gilbert explains that "some people have found it strange that Forrest Reid, who had strong spiritual affinities with ancient Greece and Renaissance Italy, should have appeared and lived in modern Belfast. To me it doesn't seem at all strange because Belfast today has a lot in common with the cities of ancient Greece and Renaissance Italy."[29]

In order to understand Reid's Hellenism, we must first ask what Greece meant to him; and, second, we must consider the extent to which Reid used the Hellenic tradition in his works. In discussing Reid's attitude toward nature, which is essential to an understanding of his mind, Russell Burlingham has explained that

> Greece represented for him all he most admired and everything on which he had most set his heart, and when he *did* discover it, the revelation enriched his whole life. There was relief, and joy too, in finding that so

much he had thought unique or unusual in himself had been shared by this
Mediterranean people thousands of years before—the love of nature, the
worship of youth, the "sense of fellowship with every scaled and furred and
feathered creature"; the vivacity of intellect, the frankness of response, and,
above all, the mythopoeic sense of wonder—"O Solon, Solon, you Hellenes
are never anything but children."[30]

The specific facets of Greek antiquity from which Reid drew his
inspiration include animism, Platonism, Humanism, mythology,
friendship, Greek sculpture and literature, time consciousness, and
dreams.[31] Even Renaissance paintings about Greek themes are
threads in the tapestry of his novels that meet the demands of his
narrative. Although Reid knew that it was impossible to recapture
the true Greek spirit, Greece is a functioning symbol used to contrast contemporaneity and antiquity.

III The Mythopoeic Imagination

To a writer whose imagination is as mythopoeic as Reid's, Greek
antiquity was a rich mine of magic, legend, myth, ritual, taboo,
nature worship, initiation ceremonies, gods and goddesses, spirits,
psychic states, supernatural phenomena, and dreams; and through
these he explored levels of reality.[32] The mythopoeic imagination
may be defined as an imaginative mode of thinking that charac-
terizes primitive man, the poet, the child, and novelists who are
visionary.[33] An imaginative mode of thinking originates in a feeling
for nature experienced as "the other" whenever rational modes are
an inadequate means of revealing spiritual truth. In the face of
existential loneliness, the mythopoeic novelist returns to a primitive
past when nature was initially perceived as a spirit, *numen*, or
anima. Thus animism becomes the means by which man communi-
cates with basic spiritual energy. As religious consciousness developed, the spirit in nature linking all levels of life in a common
bond was anthropomorphized as Ge, Mother Earth, or Demeter. In
Reid's *Demophon: A Traveller's Tale*, Demeter functions as this
life-giving source.

To explain the congruence between primitive Greek cognitive
processes and his own myth-making faculty, Reid quotes from R. W.
Livingstone, a scholar in Classical studies, to support his own views:
Everywhere the Greek "carried his passion for humanizing
things. . . . Inanimate nature became not merely animate, but hu-

man. The Greek could not think of rivers without their river-gods, or of sun and moon apart from their divinities. Naiads live in springs and are the authors of their clearness; Dryads are the tree-spirits that die when the tree is felled. A sudden fright seizes some shepherds as they feed their flock on the hillside; it was Pan who peered out at them from among the rocks."[34]

Since Reid could find no peace in the diversity of Christian creeds, in the mysticism of the East, in the "proofs" of the Society for Psychical Research, in the dogmatism of Roman Catholicism, or in Hebraism, he discovered in animism, which was compatible with his personal beliefs, the source of man's initial harmony with nature. Successive stages in the development of Reid's religious consciousness are revealed as he probes the origin and growth of anthropomorphism to explain his belief in animism:

I believe in religion, in so far as it is the symbol of an ideal. But no farther, for I also believe that the letter killeth. Man has made God—many Gods indeed—in his own image—I have made one myself. Therefore it is not surprising that these Gods should differ, since some have been conceived in fear and others in love and admiration. All are human, but that does not necessarily mean that none is divine. And again I am speaking in human terms, for our conception of divinity is of a perfected humanity existing out of space, out of time, and above all out of the body with its animal needs and desires. What is left is a naked spiritual energy. Yet is that God? Not the God we want, so we re-endow him with certain human qualities— sympathy, compassion, goodness—which may have no existence outside our own minds.[35]

If animism reconfirmed his belief in spirit, it also contrasted the commercialism of Belfast with the beauty of the surrounding countryside.

Reid is among other modern novelists whose imagination is haunted by a sense of time.[36] Since his mode of thinking is animistic, he captures time's rhythms by employing the seasonal changes in which spring and summer herald the joy of nature's resurrection that follows the autumn and winter of fruition and decay. Because clock and calendar time conflict with timelessness, the waxing and the waning of the moon become the background for psychological development as his boy heroes cross the threshold to adolescence. As with Alain-Fournier, Reid's youths' maturation unfolds in another landscape represented as "a garden of eternal Summer, of peace, happiness, and freedom of restraint of any law."[37] In this ideal geography, life that is spontaneous, instinctive, and uninhibited recalls the "vague vistas of a life continuous with our own, beckoning and inviting, yet eluding our present."[38] To bring ancient and modern time into harmony in his fiction, Reid draws on the pastoral tradition of Theocritus[39] and on the sixth Pythian Ode of Pindar[40] as literary symbols of an earthly paradise that corresponds to the beauty of the Irish countryside, the Lagan River, the Mourne Mountains, and Ballycastle by the sea.

In such an animistic world view, no separation exists between natural and supernatural, subject and object; for man, animals, birds, plants, insects, are integral parts of one "tremendous whole." Because Reid loved animals, his novels rarely fail to note their presence. He believed that a child should have a pet, preferably a dog (several of his own appear in his novels), that faithfulness in animals creates a bond not easily broken, and that animals are often more dependable than certain people. Cruelty in any form, whether as vivisection or simply as man's cruelty to furred skin, he abhorred. He also believed that instinct was often a truer guide in the pursuit of truth than intellect—and far more reliable.

IV   *Remembrance of Things Past*

From *The Kingdom of Twilight* to *Peter Waring*, the extent of Plato's influence on Reid is evidenced by sources cited in the novels. As his technique develops, his thinking becomes more genuinely Platonic and allusions almost disappear. In Plato's dual world of permanence and flux, Reid anchors the philosophical framework within which he explores a search for goodness, beauty, and truth through the eyes of an adolescent boy. The idea of preexistence becomes the symbol of innocence lost when experience brings change and evil. By drawing on prenatal memory, he accounts for emotions and intuitions otherwise inexplicable by reason and science. The archetypal reservoir of Plato's world of ideas is fused with Jung's archetypes of human experience to explain both the instinct and the "forms of behavior" manifest in recurrent patterns of the psyche's activity.[41] From Plato's *Symposium*, Diotima's ladder of love metaphor translates as Reid's concept of friendship between master and pupil as exemplified in Socrates whose genius for friendship "did not take the form of a narrow attachment to a single individual, but flowed out freely in every direction."[42]

The ideal of friendship portrayed in each of Reid's novels is based on Plato's *Lysis*, the *Phaedrus*, and the *Symposium*. In the relationship of Socrates to the youth of the Academe, Reid found his ideal, which is kept ideal in his novels. With Socrates, he believed that there can be no friendship among the evil; and, to Reid, "a life without friendship was like a world without sun."[43] Since friendship is largely male oriented both in Greek antiquity and in Reid's novels, it is used as the means to portray youth's awakening to knowledge and authenticity. Because the world of Reid's characters is apolitical, his concept of friendship recalls Epicurus's idea of friendship as an end in itself, which is wisdom.[44] By locating his sources in the Platonic dialogues, however, feeling for a friend is to Reid the starting point in a series of steps forward by which man is "raised to that expanse of beauty which is intelligible Being, and beyond that, to the One which unifies all the intelligibles."[45] He asserts that he knows of nothing higher than friendship.

In the Humanism of Socrates and Greek philosophy, Reid found sanction for his concept of happiness and the good life. In his thinking, happiness means self-fulfillment according to capacity, need, and nature. For happiness to be enjoyed in the present life, relationships should not be restricted by Puritanical inhibition, social shibboleths, or orthodox concepts of sin. A life hereafter, with rewards and punishments as taught by Christianity, was foreign to Reid's way of thinking. What he admired about his friend John McBurney, whom he ironically calls a "pagan," was his ability to face death unafraid. In this respect, Reid thought McBurney more courageous than Samuel Johnson, a Christian who lived in mortal fear of death.[46] As a Humanist, Reid believed in the natural virtues, particularly in his own kind of goodness that was based on the teachings of Socrates rather than on those of St. Paul.[47] In R. W. Livingstone's *The Greek Genius* he found his ideas corroborated.[48] When Reid treats the conflict of good and evil in exceptionally sensitive persons, he shows that goodness can be attained only when evil is faced and overcome. In his writing, Humanism as a way of life stands in sharp contrast to asceticism; for Reid's attitude toward celibacy and asceticism as life-denying forces predates current ecumenism on these very subjects and shows the influence of Anatole France.

In Reid's esthetic, the sister arts of painting, sculpture, and music enhance and deepen a novelist's spiritual vision, a view he shared with Joseph Conrad.[49] Allusions to Greek sculptures that portray young boys as the spirit of youth are central symbols in at least three of his novels. The fragmentary statue of Hermes in *Uncle Stephen*, an antique version of the Spinario in *The Garden God*, and the Hermes of Praxiteles in *Brian Westby*—"young men on the Parthenon frieze riding in proud humility"—become the ideal of youth he tried to capture in fiction.[50] Like Joseph Conrad, Reid believed that the fine arts of music, painting, and sculpture were testaments to the survival of spirituality in a materialistic world.

Between Reid and Walter Pater a striking correspondence appears in their taste for Renaissance and Romantic paintings on Greek themes. Botticelli's "Birth of Venus," Watteau's "Embarquement pour Cythère," Giorgione's "Fête Champêtre," and Giotto's "Mourning Demeter" represented the height of artistic perfection; for they surpassed Christian paintings of Madonnas or realistic representations of Christ crucified.[51] Reid's creative imagination also fed on the Greek mythology as intensely as Keats absorbed Lemprière and Tooke. The image of rural Pan that Reid associated with music, and Hermes, the guardian of boys, are controlling symbols in his novels.

V *Dreams and the Creative Process*

Dreams are of as much significance to Reid's vision as they were to primitive Greeks who believed in their gods because they had seen them in dreams[52] His use of dreams and dream technique serves several purposes. By means of them he structures, for example, an Elysian garden as an ideal world more desirable than the present world of violence, ugliness, and crass materialism; for his belief in a spiritual world is built upon his hope for a spiritual revolution. Moreover, he uses dreams to explain his creative process by reference to a dream collaborator, a technique which is similar to Ingmar Bergman's theory of creativity. In the closing chapters of *Private Road*, Reid explains his use of a dream collaborator working with him on the theme of a little boy lost. The first dream contains a princess drowned, as a sleeping boy is carried aloft by the dreamer; the second records a lost boy from the "unlettered class" later found in real life by the dreamer; in the third, a small naked boy, holding an urn in an exotic landscape, is translated into *Uncle Stephen*. Reid calls the latter a "dream story of metamorphosis composed in sleep—or lived."[53]

To the author of *Young Tom*, who wrote his novel over a period of two years, his hero became so real as to be visible in his room or on the street. Reid felt that "either Tom passes out of the world to come to me, or . . . I was going to him."[54] The subconscious mind of the dreamer is a participant in the conscious fictional rendering of a "real" boy who is also a dreamer. When writing *Uncle Stephen*, he drew upon J. W. Dunne's concept of serial time to explore time-traveling in dreams. Reid's dream psychology is closer to Ralph Waldo Emerson's than to that of Sigmund Freud in a shared belief that "our character is reflected in dreams and particularly those aspects of it which do not appear in our manifest behavior."[55] To establish the difference betwee the every-day world and the dream world, Reid uses Heraclitus of Ephesus to position two worlds in conflict: "They that are awake have one world in common, but of the sleeping each turns aside into a world of his own."[56] In the process of recreating the dream, Reid evinces neither "conscious irritability" nor a strived for effect. With firm control of technique, he shapes the world of youth and goodness wherein the spirit, as the creative essence of life, rejects whatever limits its upward progress. In reliving his own childhood, he captures moments of happiness as he arrests and fixes the permanent against the flux of time through the mode of Romantic Realism. To deepen his meaning, Hellenism is the bridge to the timelessness of his thought.

VI *Promethean Visionaries*

Opening on the threshold of existentialism, Reid's Hellenism finds a firm footing in the Ulster countryside, and dances in quiet, uninterrupted rhythms to the pipes of Pan. Beneath Reid's apostasy from orthodox religion and his choice of a private road, there is an echo of St. Augustine's soul-haunting search for God to satisfy cosmic loneliness; but for Reid no traditional concept of divinity is adequate. In St. Augustine, Albert Camus, Herman Hesse, and Reid, their yearning for unity reveals their discontent with the fragmentation of society and self.

To understand Reid's significance, we must consider the multiple meanings he asserts through his use of Greece as an integrating symbol of his values. In the beginning, he establishes an ideal geography of another country based on images from Theocritus to correlate with and give verisimilitude to the landscape of Northern Ireland—but to extend beyond its national boundaries to the world. Within this framework, he reflects the human dilemma through the conflicts that his characters encounter. The syndrome then focuses on man against society in an attempt to be himself as an individual and as a nonconformist whether in life style or in religious beliefs. In fantasy, Reid builds an ideal democracy of spirit and conscience as his hope for future generations. His Utopian scheme is the most moral of worlds where each person lives according to his nature, where nonviolence replaces war, and where happiness is possible when man lives in harmony with nature. His kingdom of peace and freedom reveals similarities to Hesse's "magical thinking" in which Hesse exchanges inner and outer reality, and explores dimensions of the marvelous, the unusual, the strange, and the different, thus placing before the reader an infinite variety of experiences which, though not average, are very human.[57]

In Reid's feeling for animals who often serve as a comment about man's failure to live up to his highest potential, Reid also has spiritual affinities with Kenneth Grahame.[58] Both believed that, because animals live by instinct according to their nature, their life is authentic, beautiful, and good—however incomplete it may be. Man is the only animal who lies, deceives, masquerades, kills his own kind, and rationalizes violence to others. If the animal kingdom seems to live more wisely than man, it suggests that man has yet to develop the higher consciousness which is cosmic.

For Reid, the ideal of the unity of man with nature demands the existence of a world where the freedom of the individual to be different takes precedence over institutional codes and over social laws which deny human rights. To achieve this ideal likewise requires a revolution in thinking about questions of good and evil, so that war and the violation of personal rights are recognized respectively as the greatest evil and as the greatest obscenity. As a result of such a view the Augustinian and the Puritan concept of sex as sin would be eradicated. If Reid's ideas anticipate the "new morality," they are also religious in the basic sense that such concepts create a bond between persons that transcends race, sex, color, belief, or nonbelief. Like Terence, he believed that to a person fully human nothing human is alien, foreign, strange, or abnormal. A careful study of Reid's meaning in his novels reveals the depth of his social consciousness on questions of minority rights, censorship, power politics, the establishment, cruelty to animals and birds, and socioeconomic inequalities. Through his visionary novels, he achieved what Dylan Thomas has called "momentary peace."

Although there are many modern Hellenists among twentieth century writers, Forrest Reid and E. M. Forster are most akin in their Promethean vision. Between Reid and Forster, his friend of thirty-five years, we find considerable correspondence in ideas, convictions, and thought. Reid's value system is analagous to Forster's Hellenism, his liberal Humanism, and his world view. Both were nonconformists, champions of human and civil rights, and passionately concerned with freedom and a free society. Recent scholarly studies by Wilfred Stone[59] Lionel Trilling,[60] and G. D. Klingopoulos[61] have explored Forster's art, thought, and Hellenism.

What Reid shares with Forster is belief in the necessity for non-violent social change, in individualism, and in democratic values. In Forster's essay "What I Believe" in *Two Cheers for Democracy*, his views on violence, war, freedom, anti-Semitism, Nazism, liberty, censorship, nonviolence, and friendship parallel Reid's ideas closely.[62] Both believed that in a world of violence and cruelty only personal relationships and friendships could be trusted; both believed in an inner light shared by the "aristocracy of the sensitive, the considerate and the plucky"[63]—an invisible community of free men like Ghandi who know that violence and force accomplish nothing that could not be achieved through nonviolent means. Both realized that violent revolutions, begun for liberation, often end as another form of tyranny; both believed in the importance of the individual over the state at a time when Fascist and Communist tyrannies demanded complete allegiance from party members. Both believed in deomocracy, its freedoms, its mechanism for public criticism of governmental activities. Both were appalled at the technological weapons in the arms race as the means for nations and persons to destroy one another.

Reid and Forster also share religious beliefs without a theology. They believed that Christianity could not provide the much-needed revolution in consciousness and in conscience that was necessary for peace in a fully human world. Within a world of "religious and racial persecution" where militant creeds warred with one another, each vigilantly guarded an inner light through the darkest days of civilization in Europe.[64]

Reid and Forster both believed that since violence has "so far never worked," art, literature, music, sculpture, graphics, and imaginative prose lie at the heart of civilization. For that reason each

believed in "art for art's sake," since the artist and the writer created
an order which preserved spiritual values in which Antigone and
Demeter played a most significant part.

VII   *Notes on the Lyrical Novel: Poetic Prose*

Reid's theory of literature as a fine art and his ideas about the
imaginative or poetic novel in particular are contained in his critical
study *The Milk of Paradise*, a work that originated as a series of talks to
young people about lyric poetry. With examples of selected Romantic poets from Blake to Walter de la Mare, he explores the lyrical
mode in prose as well as in poetry. Although his method is to focus
on Poe's definition of poetry as "the rhythmical creation of beauty,"
he extends this concept to prose writers whose words reveal "the
spirit dwelling within" as Coleridge had done before him. To illustrate his meaning, he contrasts Thomas Hardy's description of
Father Time in *Jude the Obscure* with Hardy's poem "Midnight on
the Great Western" to show that there is more poetry in the prose
than in the verse.

By poetic prose, Reid meant prose that had a subtle rhythm
closely akin to music, a quality not just the exclusive property of
literature but one found in the sister arts and, of course, in nature:

The sound of the waves on the sea-shore, a landscape seen in a certain
lighting, a group of children gathered in the street at dusk round the glow-
ing brazier of a night-watchman—all or any of these may produce in us a
particular state of mind we instinctively call poetic, and however vague,
loose, and unphilosophic our words may be, they allude to something
real—a mysterious element which somehow fertilizes a seed in the receptive mind, and gives that seed the power of growth.[65]

To Reid, poetry is "nearly as old as mankind," is unaffected by
changes in fashion and style, is as individual as one's inspiration, and
is diametrically opposed to a group style where members imitate
one another. With Shelley, he believed that poetry "turns all things
to loveliness: It strips the veil of familiarity from the world, and lays
bare the naked and sleeping beauty, which is the spirit of its forms."
With Carlyle, he found that the effect of poetry on readers was
closely akin to music as a "kind of inarticulate, unfathomable
speech, which leads us to the edge of the Infinite and lets us for a
moment gaze into that!" With Yeats, Reid agreed that poetry is

"essentially a touch from behind a curtain," a theory substantially different from Arnold's belief in poetry as a criticism of life.[66]

The quality of the mysterious—the something more suggested than is actually said, communicated in some secret way of spirit to spirit—is the essentiality that Reid demanded from literature of power and that he himself achieved in his major novels. The sense of mystery acts upon the "innate imaginative sensitiveness" that, on a simpler level, the child often shares with the poet, "a gift of receptivity . . . which like an ear for music, though it can be developed and educated, it cannot be acquired by study."[67] Reid found this gift in Wordsworth and Thomas Hardy, both masters in the pastoral tradition, and in Emily Brontë and Seumas O'Kelley of whom he wrote in *Retrospective Adventures*.

In summarizing his personal view of poetry as a necessary dimension of imaginative literature, he quotes from the *Autobiography* of John Stuart Mill about the difference between the poetry of a poet and that of a cultivated but not naturally poetic mind. Of the latter, Mill wrote: "With however bright a halo the thought may be surrounded and glorified, the thought itself is always the conspicuous object; while the poetry of a poet is Feeling itself, employing thought only as the medium of its expression."[68] Reid's ideas about the poetical character of imaginative fiction are similar to Herman Hesse's theory of the novel as a disguised lyric used to explain the "experimentations of poetic spirits to express their feeling of self and the world."[69] In *The Lyrical Novel*, Ralph Freedman defines this genre as "the paradoxical submersion of narrative in imagery and portraiture" that has opened up "ranges of metaphoric suggestiveness that could not have been achieved by purely narrative means."[70]

When Reid wrote his critical study of Yeats in 1915, the Irish poet had not yet written his greatest poems; and he therefore had to confine his interpretation to the early and middle period, ending with 1914. As a creative critic, Reid abstracted from Yeats's work qualities that accounted for its originality and uniqueness. In the conclusion to *W. B. Yeats. A Critical Study*, Reid mentions the critical methods of Walter Pater and Arthur Symons that influenced his approach to evaluation of prose, poetry, and drama. His criticism may be defined as literary "appreciation," a process whereby the critic, in Pater's words, expands the artist's work "to the full measure of intention" in order to discover not only its highest value and uniqueness but also its faults and failures. The purpose of such criticism is to awaken the reader to an "eager curiosity" and enthusiasm for the work that the critic introduces to the reader. The danger of this approach, that it is considerably subjective, has been indicated by Russell Burlingham in his study of Reid. On the other hand, the method has value because it shows the way in which Reid extends the concept of poetry to embrace forms of fiction and drama. His criticism becomes an exploration of the lyrical element in narrative or drama—its metaphor and its suggestiveness which Reid and also Walter de la Mare call "otherness," or a meaning beyond the explicit. Freedman, Reid, and de la Mare discuss the lyrical dimension of narrative writing that extends, amplifies, and intensifies the meaning of fiction. Whereas Freedman's approach centers on the narrative technique of the lyrical novelist, both Reid and de lar Mare focus on the importance of metaphor and resonance in the art of language.

In 1935, Walter de la Mare delivered before the British Academy the Wharton Lecture on English Poetry which bore the title "Poetry in Prose."[71] The substance of the lecture is to show that prose as well as poetry can capture the truth of the imagination. If this monograph may be used as a stage against which we can then place Reid's methodology in his early study of Yeats and in his later study of de la Mare, it may help the reader see Reid's approach more clearly. Both Reid and de la Mare agree that, for a novelist of poetic temperament and individuality of mind, his more difficult task is the finding of words to establish a "pattern and design" to embody both intention and maximum meaning. Words must be selected not only to function efficiently, but to duplicate a melody corresponding to their sound and intonation, which in prose as in poetry depends upon modulation. Drawing upon examples of words that resemble "a printed melody in music," de la Mare shows that not only "prose, but ordinary speech is rhythmic." To support this thesis, he first uses an example from the short story "Arabesque" by Somerset Maugham and then lines from a debate by Rose Macaulay that by accent and stress are poetry. In Elizabethan prose, de la Mare finds extensive examples of poetic style characterized by "rhythm, cadence, color, and rapidity"—a poetic style in which words echo sense. In conclusion, de la Mare states that "the realm of poetry extends far beyond . . . the confines of verse" as Shelley's definition of poetry also clearly shows.

In *W. B. Yeats. A Critical Study*, Reid includes a discussion of the early poems, the later lyrics, and "Plays for the Irish Theatre." A chapter about Yeats's philosophy reveals Reid's criteria for imaginative prose style as he explores Yeats's genius in the lyrical mode. He begins with the concept that all great art is characterized by nobility, dignity, and tenderness, qualities that natural, rhythmical language may reveal when prose is artistically written. Words, Reid maintained, must convey "a revelation of a hidden life," to be found in novels such as Emily Brontë's *Wuthering Heights* though not in William Makepeace Thackeray's *Vanity Fair*. The early Yeats, like Emily Brontë, used words to capture emotions eternal in humanity against a background of nature as a "transparent veil" through which eternal powers shine. Reid believed that Yeats achieved his effects through his prosody founded on what Robert Bridges later called "the natural speech stress and a variety of modulation" that resulted in a "natural speech intonation."[72]

When submitted to an oral test, Yeats's language in both prose and poetry revealed a lyric genius. In his early poetry, he achieved an originality of pagan feeling, mythopoeia, and spiritualization of nature, qualities he lost when he reworked his lyrical drama *The Land of Heart's Desire* to conform to the demands of the stage. Reid believed that even Yeats's short story "Costello the Proud" and the stories in *The Secret Rose* were more artistically perfect for their naturalness and verbal rhythm, or what he called their "inwardness" and "lyricism," than later stories like "Rose Alchemica," "The Tables of the Law," and "The Adoration of the Magi." The later stories were too consciously contrived, too imitative of the occult doctrines of Macgregor Mathers and the Hermetic Order of the Golden Dawn, and too heavily weighted with Mallarméism. The inwardness and the lyricism that Reid regards as basic to originality are neither the product of schools nor learned by imitations that detract from the original and make common what is rare. At the basis of art, he found a cosmic loneliness that imaginative prose conveys.

Although Reid sympathized with Yeats's desire to bring poetic drama to the Irish stage, he doubted that the subtlety and allusiveness characteristic of Maeterlinck's *The Blue Bird* could find receptivity with Irish audiences so enmeshed in the quarrel between politics and religion. Reid found a parallel for his skepticism about poetic drama for Ireland in the failure of Euripides and Sophocles to be accepted in their time by the average citizen of Greece. In the-

style of Jeremy Taylor and Anatole France, he found natural
rhythmic language characterized by a richness of metaphor and
suggestiveness. Freed from conscious rhetorical ornament, their
style revealed a depth of feeling and insight expressed in "simple,
sensuous and compassionate" prose. In Reid's esthetic, words must
have pictorial as well as musical quality; images must be connected
to ideas as body is to soul so that picture and scene are transfused by
the idea but indistinguishable from it. If the image is functional, it
will then "evoke a train of associations haunted by unseen presences . . . wrapped in mystery, . . . and brooded over by the atmosphere of the soul."[73]

The concept of fiction as revelation that Reid found so abundant in
the early Yeats is also described in *Walter de la Mare: A Critical
Study* to account for his originality.[74] For purposes of analysis, our
focus centers on Reid's discussion of the poetic prose of de la Mare's
The Three Mulla-Mulgars (later retitled *The Royal Monkeys*); *The
Return,* a novel of the occult; and *Memoirs of a Midget.* From these
works, Reid once again selects examples of de la Mare's imaginative
fiction to show the luminous quality of his art. Reid attributes de la
Mare's success to his use of interior landscapes that were distanced
from him by writing in novel form. In each work, where the hero
masks the writer's intentions, he becomes the autonomous "other"
in whose world the author's inner landscape is mirrored. If, like his
heroes, he knew hints of immortality, he also knew that the ugliness
and evil of the world threatened to destroy the purity of the primal
Eden. Whether in poetry for children or in fiction, de la Mare's
rich, varied music—the rhythm and melody of his language—
achieves what Reid calls a mysterious undermeaning, "whispering
out of the depths, gripping our imagination, throwing open every
door and window to vision and dream" (33). His prose is the stuff of
fantasy—romantic, brooding, and haunting in its melody—and it is
as unusual as it is artistic.

In Reid's classification, *The Three Mulla-Mulgars* is primarily a
lyrical novel that has the magic of Lewis Carroll's *Alice in Wonderland.* In its mixture of fantasy and realism, the geography and spirit
of the borders of the forest of Munza-Mulgar come alive as Thumb,
Thimble, and Nod set out to find their father, Seelem, Prince of
the Valley of Tishnar, in the Kingdom of Assasimmon from
which each is exiled. On their exciting adventures before reaching
Tishnar, they meet extraordinary people and animals. With their
wonderstone to help them, and the leadership of the brave little

Nod who never gives up or gives in, they escape many perilous paths. " 'Tishnar is a very ancient word in Munza, and means that which cannot be thought about in words, or told or expressed. . . .' " So all the wonderful " 'secret and quiet world beyond the Mulgars' lives . . .' " is Tishnar—" 'wind and stars, too, and the sea and the endless unknown . . .' " (119). This "world beyond" is the world within, a world "remote as the stars . . . bathed in an earthly atmosphere." Tishnar is both a place and a spirit. To Reid, Tishnar is the Spirit of the Good that recalls to his mind the beautiful hymn to Demeter, an archetypal pattern of hearth and home. Its dimensions are "matter of truth not matter of fact," and they reflect as "first hand knowledge and experience . . . the life of its writer" (119). Within this romantic odyssey, courage, moral integrity, and love bridge the gap between two worlds.

The qualities of suggestibility, diaphanété, and resonance constitute "the meaning beyond" that Reid also found in *The Return*, a lyrical story of the occult that won for de la Mare the de Polignac prize. Beneath the explicit meaning of the narrative, Reid caught a hint of "spiritual upheaval such as might be produced by any violent emotional crisis, religious or otherwise" (131). A summary reveals that Arthur Lawford is possessed by the spirit of a French Casanova, Nicholas Sabathier, in a struggle that explores psychologically its hero's moral dilemma. Within Lawford's predicament, de la Mare reveals what Reid calls a vision of a "haunted darkly lovely world," and a "far off desolate longing for home and childhood" (140) that is its world within and the world beyond, although frustration is the note on which the story ends. In this novel, Reid also finds that "a passionate spiritual beauty" is its outstanding quality; and it is achieved through de la Mare's tight control of images and scenes that induce a mood of receptivity in the reader as he responds to the vibrations of "the mind behind the work." Its tension derives from the prolonged duel between the "haunter and the haunted," and between the ordinary, practical wife Sheila, whose life has been ruled by what others think, and her husband, whose love for a young girl shakes the roots of a marriage relationship in which love is dead. Strangeness added to beauty in the midst of middle class domesticity is the dimension that Reid discovers in de la Mare's very human story.

The height of de la Mare's originality and uniqueness Reid sees in *Memoirs of a Midget*, a novel brilliantly objective in its portrayal of the individual against society. Miss M and Mr. Anon, the midgets, represent the "different" regarded "generically and philosophically" while the other characters represent the norm. The tragic vision in the novel lies in the realization that society can find no place for the two midgets. Mr. Anon turns his back on the world and lives as if on a desert island; Miss M refuses to be crushed by the senseless weight of middle class hypocrisy; but in the end, the weight of convention prevails, and Mr. Anon is the sacrificial victim.

As a novel of modern life told from an unusual angle, *Memoirs of a Midget* creates an illusion of reality from beginning to end. Reid's criticism sends the reader back to the original work where, through Miss M's eyes, he sees and feels the hurts and snubs to which she and Mr. Anon are continually subjected. Never for one moment is the accident of Miss M's physical abnormality forgotten, nor is her closeness to animals omitted. If she is repulsed by servants and certain other humans, a little pasha whom she meets on a train instantly falls in love with her. Miss M lives for the reader through Reid's criticism and his choice of selected passages because her thoughts, feelings, and emotions, though rarefied, are "absolutely, deeply human" as de la Mare has drawn her character and as Reid has probed de la Mare's technique. Even the autobiographical form is strictly controlled as Miss M relates the story of her life; and, since Miss M shares the genius of de la Mare, moments in her autobiography reveal "a whispered echo from beyond" (191). Without sentimentaility or self-pity, she watches the world she is "up against" and sees individuals as they are (except for Fanny Bowater, whom she can never understand).

Mr. Anon is also a dimension of the "other." Although he is "a dwarf, a hunchback, a tragic human failure," he is also to Reid a "spirit, the spirit of the woods of Wanderslore, the dark and passionate spirit of tragic love" (193–94) whom Miss M never really knows until his fall from the trapeze in her stead brings home the meaning of his love and magnanimity. Through her eyes, the reader sees the cruelty of the world to those outside its norms, and knows as she knows that one need not fear the ghosts of the dead but should fear living mortals of limited minds and unsympathetic hearts. As she broods on what the gift of life implies and thanks God for the happiness and the misery of being alive, she symbolizes the universal irony of life in which love for another is so often wasted. She is one of life's born losers, but she brings the greatest loss to herself when she sends Mr. Anon into the circus ring where jeers, hoots, and insults are a prelude to his death fall. Though she lives to write her *Memoirs*, she obviously found "nothing significant in the events of her later life that seemed worth recording" (204).

To the small stream of writers in the lyrical mode in which Reid places Yeats and Walter de la Mare, he himself properly belongs since he embraced the challenge of "reconciling the inner and the outer with each other and with the exigencies of art."[75] If his criticism reveals his ability to capture and to elucidate the poetic qualities in imaginative writing, his novels bear testimony to his achievement.

CHAPTER 3

Pipes of Pan in Belfast:
The Early Novels (1904–1912)

FROM Reid's *The Kingdom of Twilight* (1904) to his *Following Darkness* (1912), he began a lifetime dedicated to a personal vision of beauty and humanity as seen through the eyes of a child or an adolescent. In each case, the boy is unusual, exceptional, precious, imaginative, and a dreamer. Although not so "normal" as Mark Twain's Tom Sawyer, he shares the rebellion against "Olympians" that is common to modern novels of adolescence. He "opts" for a better, unrestricted, more natural world; and he grows more human as he discovers himself through a friend. By means of friendship, Reid explores unusual states of mind, feeling, and consciousness as his heroes respond to nature, to animals, to evil, and to beauty. It is perhaps safe to say that each of Reid's novels is a minor symphony on the same theme—youth—since his emphasis never changes nor does his interest flag.

Although he considered his beginnings "false starts," his early novels are important because they reveal the direction that his future novels take. Inasmuch as the supernatural was inseparable from his conception of reality, we must expect to find unusual "happenings." Because Hellenism shapes and colors his vision of reality, we must see the magician at work. Time past may become time present, a dream may recall the Elysian Fields, or Pan may be heard in the hills; for nothing is impossible if the heart is willing and cares. Since Reid does not belong to a school or to a coterie, he must be accepted on his own terms.

I The Kingdom of Twilight

Willy Trevelyan, the hero of Reid's first novel, *The Kingdom of Twilight*, reflects that " 'We are in the twilight of our world, . . . the spirit of sunlight no longer, as in the golden days of Athens, shines through our work, our art, our life. Our beauty is

54

built up of mystery and silence—a beauty of pale women seen somewhere in the shadow-land.' "[1] In this statement, Reid establishes a contrast between the antique and modern world as the controlling principle of this novel. Quotations on the titlepage from Ernest Dowson[2] and Paul Verlaine[3] position his rejection of the esthetic creed of the Symbolists, for Reid's use of the pastoral tradition of Theocritus and the philosophy of Plato become in this novel functioning symbols of a "psychic reality that has little to do with exterior reality."[4]

The theme of *The Kingdom of Twilight* is the formative influence of evil and good, of profane and sacred love, on the mind of Willy Trevelyan in his quest for beauty and certainty throughout his life. Although Reid carries Willy through middle age, this novel is predominantly a study of adolescence, following the traditional pattern of rebellion against family, middle class environment, education, and religion. As he grows to sexual awareness, searching for fulfillment through sensations, disillusionment besets him at every turn. Only in literature can he find confirmation of a more natural, harmonious world as an alternative to the present one.

From the outset, Willy Trevelyan is of different clay from most boys. As seen through his cousin Eva's eyes, Willy is supersensitive and somewhat "peculiar"; he does not belong to the world of ordinary people but lives in a world of his own creation—a private world; and, like the youths in Pater's novels, Willy's nature is "rare, exquisite, fine—as fine as that of a Sèvres vase . . ." (30). To Eva, he is an enigma: a strange, melancholy boy with a "hint of an inherited strain of refined animalism" about him and "an almost diseased hatred of the commonplace" (6–7). To Mrs. Gower, Willy's aunt, the boy would never be anything but a "superfastidious dilet-tante, . . . an amateur of delicate and rare things" (31). To his father, the Reverend Arthur Trevelyan, Willy is a "problem child" who needs to be chastised on occasion for his willfulness and disobedience. Nick Grayson, his best friend, sees Willy as a mysterious and, at times, disquieting personality. From this multiple point of view, Willy's artistic temperament is definitely established.

The plot is relatively simple: a series of everyday episodes serve as the framework for the values that the story asserts. Willy Trevelyan, an imaginative, sensitive boy—a dreamer—is expelled from his English boarding school under mysterious circumstances.

Back home in Belfast, his uncongenial surroundings, his antagonism toward his father, his hatred of the Puritanical religion of his family, and his loneliness lead him to withdraw into a world of his own imagination that is haunted by visions of beauty. As he develops physically, he is initiated into sex through reading erotic tales. Because of his loneliness and his inability to concentrate in school, he is placed in the tea trade by his father.

Unhappy in this commercial and philistine world, Willy launches upon an extensive reading program in "dangerous French books" that include Charles Baudelaire's *Les Fleurs du Mal* and Joris Karl Huysmans' *Là-Bas;* he gets intoxicated in a "pub"; and he is overwhelmed by a desire to die. Since he has rejected Presbyterianism as narrow and static, Willy searches for comfort in a spiritualistic seance, which he finds repulsive, and in the ritual and litany of the Catholic Church, which, while satisfying his senses, leaves his spirit dull and disquieted. When by chance he meets the strangely beautiful Mrs. Urquardht, he has an affair with her that ultimately leads to marriage. His separation from his wife, his subsequent struggle for survival in London, the death of their son Prosper, and his final and complete rejection of Christianity in favor of Greek "paganism" form the last section of the novel.

Having placed the characters against the background of his own Belfast, Reid then selected from Greek literature and philosophy those themes that compare and contrast the values of modern and ancient time. The earthly paradise of Homer's Elysian Fields becomes the geography of the "other country." Colored by his Romantic imagination, the landscape functions as Willy's desire for freedom from the restraints of social and religious law. Lush Oriental beauty is superimposed on Homer's simple, direct description; for in Willy's land "flowers grew in marvellous profusion" with "no gardener to tell one which to pluck and which to leave alone" (1). Watered by a stream that had mingled with Lethe, its magic property lulls things to sleep. In the river of forgetfulness, he would blot out any remembrance of the past deeds and the darkness of which the self was conscious. All other landscapes gain "an extraordinarily exotic beauty," a beauty possessing something of the "fleeting, the indescribable and elusive loveliness of a dream" (2). Dream as wish fulfillment represents a longing for a personal paradise that emanates from Willy's dissatisfaction with life as it is.

Since a "pagan" world demands a "pagan" ethic, Willy's dream

world is "not very Christian, yet not all pagan, after the Greek
manner" (2). His paganism is "not necessarily immoral, yet
assuredly not very moral; one, rather, where questions such as these
were left delightfully alone; where fauns and other charming
creatures, part human, part animal, part divine, might live very well
their delicate, untroubled lives, in dreamy sunshine, without fear of
interruption" (2). As an amoral world, it excludes no one human
from its realm; and even the children of pleasure with whom Willy
identifies are free from religious and social restrictions. To feel
beauty in intensity, erotic French novels feed his sexual obsessions
and influence his dreams. In a Kafkaesque nightmare, he is victim of
the "Moonlight Madonna's" thirst for blood as the body of a naked
youth is being sacrificed on an altar before her while choir boys
chant a triumphal hymn of love. The dreamer suddenly finds
himself part of the procession, naked, alone, and powerless to flee
her attraction:

And now he felt the warmth of her hot breath upon his face. Nearer and
nearer: he was under the light, now, of her hard, burning eyes. Then, with
almost a scream of terror, he saw her sway slowly toward him; felt, as he
passed beneath the throne, her lips fasten upon his. But already his fear was
gone. He stood quite still, a sharp, exquisite sweetness running in rapidly
augmenting waves through his body as she pressed him to her, and, at
length, dying away in a delicious languor as, between her parted lips, she
drank up his life (52).

Thematically, Reid uses the vampire motif and the search for a
divine friend to orchestrate the conflict between modern and
ancient customs and practices that govern human relationships.[5]
What clearly emerges is the image of women who dominate men
through marriage, and this situation contrasts with the male
friendships in antique societies that are sanctioned in life and
glorified in art. Indeed, the image of a naked youth sacrificed to a
vindictive goddess functions as a foreshadowing of Willy's
unfortunate marriage to Mrs. Urquardht. Simultaneously, it reveals
Willy's subconscious fear of being consumed by sex. Mrs.
Urquardht, who symbolizes sensuality, enters Willy's world just at
the point where he has seemingly resolved his struggle; and the
scarlet poppies of Proserpine that she carries on one occasion are
emblems of her fatal power.

In contrast to Mrs. Urquardht, Nick Grayson's spirituality is revealed in a series of expanding images. Nick is Willy's ideal of spiritual beauty, the godlike beauty of Grecian youth. He is "pure like a painting of Leonardo's"; he resembles the young Ion of Euripides, a youthful priest in the temple of Diana. In a reverie, Willy sees Nick in a "long procession of Greek boys" on a "crocus strewn path" in the "shadow of a grove" (73). Consciously to Willy, Nick becomes a symbol of spiritual light that is "the fountainhead of the Platonic philosophy" (79). Like a Greek temple, Nick's spirit is "broad and fair and open to the sky" (Apollonian), with no "veiled secret shrines, labyrinthine passages and closed doors" (Dionysian). Nick becomes Willy's teacher as they explore the spiritual way in Plato's *Symposium,* and Nick instructs Willy in the relationship of beauty to truth as the ultimate of the philosopher's search: "To see that beauty, to have it before you" is the end of life and the motivation of conduct (141). Through Willy's friendship with Nick as the angel of light, Reid develops the growth of Willy's creative imagination. A rose becomes a symbol of fire "in whose flaming heart . . . the forms of gods and men move, more beautiful than any men or women he had ever beheld" (92). The development of Willy's artistic temperament is more important to Reid than a detailed portrayal of Willy's unhappy marriage to Mrs. Urquardht.

The confessional nature of this novel closely identifies Reid and his hero in their search for religious values and in their dedication to writing. The novel reflects an image of a writer whose mode of thinking is Platonic; and, given this identity, the novel results in a self-portrait. First, Willy begins to write poetry by imitating the Greek anthologists; for when he fancies himself in love with Cousin Eva, he quotes Sappho. Second, in his search for an ideal republic or "the City of God," he adopts Athens, his symbol of the Golden Age, where "Socrates talked to Phaedrus" on the immortality of the soul and where the shepherds of Theocritus play their pipes (163). Third, he gradually arrives at a belief in a "world soul" in which "the present is but the past awakened to a deeper self-consciousness" (164).

Since dreams "are the real world," the function of the imaginative writer is to make "the outer material world subservient to the inner spiritual world, to make the sensible things around us bend to one's soul" (166). To find permanence, Willy must follow the spirit of paganism: "In good and evil I must seek it, in dreaming and in waking, in heaven and in hell" (167). When his efforts to write a pastoral play on Triptolemos and Demophon are frustrated by perpetual intrusions, Willy recalls the idyll of Theocritus in which a girl, forsaken by her lover and kneeling beneath a moonlit sky, plies her magic wheel to draw her lover back. The image portrays the subsequent dissolution of his marriage as well as his preference for nonphysical relationships. From his study of Greek literature, his discovery of animism and humanism free him from Presbyterianism with its Puritan ethic.

When Willy's nine year old son Prosper asks his father "What is a pagan?", the answer synthesizes Trevelyan's religious and esthetic philosophy, a reply that echoes Reid's *Apostate:*

He is a boy for whom the world is full of beautiful gods. . . . There is the great god Pan who lives in the meadows and in the woods and among the mountains; and who pipes in the shade while the little fauns dance and sing. And it is he who watches the ships as they come slowly across the "wine dark" sea. And there is Poseidon who lives far down under the waves, and whose white horses and chariot you can see on stormy days; and Demeter who walks in the yellow corn-fields and helps the reapers; and her daughter Persephone who stands among the sleepy poppies; and Hermes the god of the fields and the ways. And there are nymphs—nymphs of all kinds—some that live in streams and ponds; and some that live in grottos; and some again, called Dryads, who are the nymphs of trees. Each Dryad lives in a particular tree, and when that tree dies, or is cut down, then the poor nymphs must die too. And there are the elves and fairies, the creatures that live in your tales, and dance under the moon. The wind is a god, and the sky is the greatest god of all; so that you are never alone. For all of them watch over you, love you and help you, both in the daytime and in the night. And you must love them, too, Prosper, and everything that is theirs and speaks of them, every tree and flower, and every little living thing, and other boys like yourself—you must never do them harm, nor think hardly of them (266–67).

The syndrome of rebellion against Christianity with an acceptance of the Greek way is a standard pattern in each of Reid's successive novels. Willy's choice of the natural, spontaneous, uninhibited order as the "ideal-real" against the drab, ugly, commonplace world of Belfast reveals the angle from which Reid sees the world.

Outwardly, *The Kingdom of Twilight* is a realistic story; but the action of the novel is contained in the interior dialogue as Willy moves through crises of self-identity in his search for a better world in which to live. If the real world is always present, it grows more tawdry and dull as Willy ages and marries. Hope for a new tomorrow is passed on to Prosper who would have been the future generation had he lived. His death does not involve the death of the dream, however, since it is already recorded in Reid's novel. Reid also makes maximum use of a world within a world in which his choice of another landscape, the Elysian Fields and Athens, serves to unite the separate aspects of religion (animism), philosophy, ethics, and esthetics into a total world picture. His sensitive treatment of the friendship theme is similar to Herman Hesse's portrait in *Demian* of the relationship of Emil Sinclair to his friend Demian. *The Kingdom of Twilight* is also a novel about the problem of the writer's attempt to record his vision. Although Willy's poems and drama never get written, Reid successfully captures the struggle of the artist against middle class society and the limitations of its outlook.

Reid was less successful in his portrayal of Mrs. Urquardht, and he knew it. She is too highly personified as vice—too obviously a "femme fatale" like Thomas Hardy's Arabella in *Jude the Obscure*. Reid is at his best in his picture of the adolescent as an imaginative youth, a prototype artist. Willy's awakening to sex through "scrofulous" French novels is dated, but his feeling of disgust with the opening behind the Japanese screen is a functional symbol of his sexual "hangups."

Henry James wrote an encouraging letter to Reid praising the "artistic fidelity and sincerity, . . . the elements of beauty" in his novel. He also noted that, despite its improportions, Reid would, no doubt, outgrow its many "aberrations." That his "young man" went to pieces at the stage where he succumbed to feminine attractions Reid knew before James mentioned it, just as he knew the limits of his range.[6] He saw, too, the inconsistency in style resulting from his use of "a vicious medium that was neither prose nor poetry in imitation of D'Annunzio and Walter Pater."[7] After the publication of the novel, Reid tried unsuccessfully to withdraw all copies from circulation.

The purple passages, the obvious dialectic, the length of descriptive passages at times interfering with the narrative, the inclusion of sources in the context, and his inability to treat of marriage do not mitigate against its spiritual dimensions. *The Kingdom of Twilight* is an important first novel for a writer whose subject is always youth, whose vision of a better world holds promise, and for whom Greek antiquity consistently shapes and forms meaning.

II The Garden God

" 'And Jonathan told him, and said, I did but taste a little honey with the end of the rod that was in mine hand, and lo, I must die.' "[8] The biblical story of Jonathan and David[9] reenforces the Greek ideal of friendship that Reid adapted to modern time to express the meaning and tragedy underlying his second novel, *The Garden God: A Tale of Two Boys* (1905).[10] This novel marks Reid's immersion in Platonic philosophy as he portrays the friendship between Graham Iddesleigh and Harold Brocklehurst that began in an English boarding school and ended in Ireland. Planned as "a realistic school story," it became a "lyrical romance" as Reid rhythmically explores states of mind and feeling in an adolescent's awakening to first love. In this respect, *The Garden God* may be compared to Ivan Turgenev's blend of "reality and beauty."[11]

Cast in the form of a reverie that establishes a mood of nostalgia for times past, Reid's story is told as a tale within a tale. The writer is the middle-aged narrator, Graham Iddesleigh, who reminisces about his childhood and youth. Following the death of his mother, Graham was reared by his father at a beautiful country estate in Ireland where his mind was nourished on Plato and Sophocles. A sensitive, imaginative only child who has no young friends, Graham dreams of an imaginary playmate and of an imaginary world of beauty. So vivid is his imagination that the myths of his reading become real, and the forest is peopled with gods and goddesses. At school in England, he meets Harold Brocklehurst, the living reality of his dream playmate, who becomes his friend. Through Harold's influence, Graham draws closer to nature, rediscovers Plato, and responds to the beauties of Greek poetry.

During the summer holidays, when Harold visits Graham at his home in Ireland, the boys are happy about their proximity to nature: they swim in the sea, hike through the hills, and discuss in youthful fashion subjects of interest to their awakening minds. One day after swimming, they play a game of Greek statues, offer prayers to Dionysius, and participate in a pagan ritual. On the way home from their outing, Harold is accidentally killed by a horse while attempting to save Graham. Harold's tragic death has such a traumatic effect on Graham that he becomes ill with a deep melancholia that affects his life and work. Thirty years later, he is the middle-aged writer whose main occupation in life is dreaming and "remembering."

The interior background for this story lies deep in Reid's early childhood. The country to which he nightly returns in dream was always the same, and a dream companion, a boy of his own age, never fails to appear. As a child, Reid lived in two worlds that were equally real. His dream world of "eternal summer and sunshine" was located in the hills, or by the sea, or in a garden where stone figures, like benevolent spirits, guarded the happiness of the young Reid and his dream companion against intrusion. The only disturbing element in the dream was the crouching panther with a human face of which he wrote in *Apostate*. This dream, he tells us, "remained *in* time," meaning that "the boy in it grew older as I myself grew older."[12]

In *The Garden God,* Graham reminisces about his childhood when he is searching for a pattern to explain his present state. He remembered that his father had brought back from his Greek travels the "chipped and broken statue of a boy in yellowish marble, . . . an antique version of a famous Spinario" (8), which he had placed in the garden. In time, the garden god became to the boy the messenger of Eros, the dream companion who stayed with him thoughout childhood. The geography of his dream world, charted from his reading in Plato, Socrates, and Greek mythology, is translated to the Irish landscape. In the whisperings of the wind and in the murmuring of the fountain he learned of "the wanderings of Odysseus, of Jason and the Golden Fleece" (10). The visible world seemed an imitation of the eternal, the "perfect beauty which lifts one's spirit to God" (12). In the natural countryside of his native Ireland, he was always happy.

Loneliness assaults Graham, the exile in his English boarding school, until he meets Harold Brockelhurst, whose physical beauty could only be compared to that of myths, the garden god, and the playmate of his dreams. Harold is the young god Pan, playing on a flute in the sunshine of a garden. When Graham tells Harold that he is his dream incarnate, Harold cannot understand Graham's private world. Through friendship, Graham reawakens to the beauty of nature, the spirit that links leaf, plant, and man together in natural harmony. Like Pater's Flavian,[13] Graham's entire being responds to the "great rhythmic chaunt of the sensuous life" (57). In the course of time, Graham remembers the legend of Dionysius, a haunting of something darker, a premonition that passed as quickly as it came. Gradually, he realizes that good and evil are not polarities but inexplicably and hopelessly tied together.

In walks with Harold through the countryside, Graham thinks of Socrates and Phaedrus walking along a stream in ancient Athens; and he prays to Pan to make the "outward and the inward man one" (65). When they swim in the sea, Graham parallels their activities to Odysseus' journeys to Circe's island, the land of the lotuseaters, or the home of Nausicaa. In the naked swimmer drying his body on the shore, Graham sees the ideal of human perfection comparable only to Greek statues. Playing a game of "statues," Graham postures Harold as a faun, a spinario, the "Adornate," the youthful Dionysius, and Leonardo's "Bacchus." Performing a mock ritual, he offers flowers to Dionysius and induces Harold to pray that the gods of Greece may accept their gifts. The image of Hippolytus immersed in the waves upsets their uneasy calm, which is later shattered by Harold's death. As the narrator reflects on the sacrifice, he knows that the belief in immortality is based on a "very simple human desire to look upon the face of a friend" (97).

Just as Reid used time as structure in *The Kingdom of Twilight*, he uses dream time in *The Garden God* to portray the repetition in the present of the past and the eternal. The antique statue of the Spinario is the controlling symbol from which Reid's meaning emanates. The story begins with the reverie of the narrator, ". . . my father was an archaeologist . . ."; it advances the theme of the cosmic and personal loneliness in an only child's desire for a playmate; it spirals with the joy in friendship discovered; it climaxes with the death of the friend; and it concludes with the denouement, the feeling of futility overpowering the narrator. Its inner structure is the music of feeling, natural as the flow of the river in whose depths the tragic ending is contained and symbolized. To support the lyrical structure, Reid uses Plato's *Symposium* to buttress the theme and move it forward; however, such dialectic support is perhaps unfortunate since it hinders at times the free flow of feeling basic to the reverie.

The Spinario also functions as the visible equivalent of beauty and pain through which Reid comments about the demands of life and art. The sculptor has captured at a fixed moment in time the beauty

of the boy's posture in the act of removing a thorn from his foot.
Where the sculptor has succeeded in rendering the beautiful in
concrete form, the narrator, from the vantage point of a middle-aged
writer, has failed. The reverie then becomes the means by which
Reid comments on the failure of the Romantic imagination to
portray adequately the "glory and the dream," the vision of a lost
paradise. The similarity between the narrator and the author, both
struggling with the problems of an imagination that is esemplastic,
necessarily involves the reconciliation of opposites: the natural and
the supernatural; the ideal and the real; the familiar and the strange.
For Reid, speaking through his narrator, the perfection of art
demands a perfection of personal life; therefore, suffering, pain, and
the experience of evil both test and strengthen the moral fibre. If
the writer listens to another drummer and answers that call, he is
destined to suffer the alienation and the figurative death of
Hippolytus. The vision of the story, however, guarantees the
survival of the ideal and reaffirms Reid's belief in immortality
through the art of writing, despite the vicissitudes of the public's
reading taste.

   The Garden God is the fictional equivalent of Reid's belief in love
as the basis for communication "of God with man. . . . The wisdom
which understands this is spiritual. . . ." Generally speaking, "all
desire of good and happiness is only the great and subtle power of
love." The Platonic concept of love, which was "extolled and
accepted as an aspect of Greek genius," involves the realization of
divine love through human relationships. Although Plato's concept
of love was "a stepping stone to higher things," Reid maintains that
he could not conceive of anything higher than friendship.[14]

   Because of the highly emotive and symbolic language, *The
Garden God* may be read as a poem organized by means of
recurrent garden imagery. The imaginary landscape of the dream is
garden-centered, and the function of the garden is to convey
timelessness and to recall the feeling associated with the primal
state of happiness. As Graham looks back, his life is like a "broad,
shady garden, an old world, a sleepy garden full of flowers sweet and
fresh" (5); in the garden itself is the antique statue; Graham's
surroundings are "beautiful" (9); magic influences are awake in the
sleepy "garden." In the rose garden, a fountain whispers tales of the
golden fleece (11); Graham's garden is a strange "meadow of
asphodel" (13). Harold is as "beautiful as an angel" (Paradisiac

theme) whom Graham knew in a "garden," and he always returned in memory to the "garden" (20). Even after Harold's death, Graham sees him in "a garden" (101). Thus the garden imagery serves as the thematic structure to portray the Theocritan landscape transposed to Northern Ireland and as background for the friendship theme that evolves throughout the novel.

The Garden God in both technique and meaning shows the influence of Pater's "The Child in the House." Graham is a "Pateresque" character who has lived the life of a hermit "with a taste for the philosophy of Epicurus and Anatole France" (2). In this poetic study of an adolescent's awakening to the meaning of life through friendship with a youth of his own age, Reid's use of a sustained point of view and of reverie show his mastery of Henry James's techniques. Although the prose is highly sensuous and uneven at times and although the dialogue is contrived, a haunting lyrical melody lies beneath the surface. Reid's ability to portray the adolescent awakening to his own identity by using the framework of "Greek" friendship to comment on human relationships that are as ancient as man is a tribute to his art and to his ability to handle time.

As a modern Hellenic tale, colored by Reid's mythopoeic imagination, this novel deserves comparison with Thomas Mann's *Death in Venice* and Herman Hesse's *Demian*. However, the mixed reception that this novel received, already discussed in Chapter 1, warrants summation: Edmund Gosse saw "the sorrow and pain" beneath the surface; to Arthur Symons, it was a poem; to an anonymous reviewer in the *Mercure de France*, its purely Platonic characteristics were worth comment; and, to Henry James, the work merited his refusal of a dedication to him in what Reid dejectedly called the "fateful letter."[15] In his next novel, *The Bracknels*, Reid again explores spiritual phenomena and unusual states of feeling in a Realistic setting; and it contains a "fantastic and lyrical tale" of the moon.

III   The Bracknels

The Bracknels: A Family Chronicle (1911),[16] intended as a Realistic novel, is dominated by an Endymion theme that both controls and colors the story. "Created by a collaborator working beneath consciousness," the story of a moon-worshipper originates in "a mysterious region of other reality."[17] The myth is the means by which Reid portrays the conflict between spiritual and materialistic values as two worlds collide. The pattern of adolescent revolt against family, religion, materialism, and violence is the outer conflict that precipitates Denis Bracknel's alienation, psychosis, and ultimate death.

Denis Bracknel, like Willy Trevelyan and Graham Iddelsleigh, is a sensitive, imaginative, not quite "normal" boy who is reared by a middle class Irish family in a bourgeois environment to which he does not seem to belong. Through the eyes of George Rusk, Denis's English tutor from Trinity College, Cambridge, the narrator sees the Bracknel family as Denis also sees them. The father is a gross, domineering, insensitive Irishman from Belfast whose success in business does not extend to his family relationships; and Denis's mother, frail, melancholy, and soul-weary, is caught between father and son. Amy, the younger sister, is attracted to Rusk, who is unable to reciprocate her feeling. The older sister May, like Denis, is gentle, intelligent, and sensitive. Alfred, the elder brother, is materialistic, aggressive, and ego-driven. Dr. Birch, a friendly physician who knows of Denis's abnormality, hopes that Rusk may help the boy achieve a healthy balance and adjust to the world as it is.

The plot is divided into a series of episodes that center around the antagonism between Mr. Bracknel and his elder son Alfred because of his father's perference for John Brooke who works in the family business. When Alfred's secret marriage to Rhoda Brooke, the adopted sister of John Brooke, is discovered, Mr. Bracknel threatens to disinherit him; but Alfred counters with blackmail since he knows that John Brooke is his father's illegitimate son. During a violent confrontation between father and son, Mr. Bracknel suffers an attack of apoplexy while Alfred stands by watching his father die. The sudden and mysterious death brings home to Denis the ugliness and violence of life. Obsessed by malignant supernatural influences, threatened by the impending departure of his tutor, and overpowered by the evil that he cannot understand, Denis takes his own life.

As for the order of events that culminate in Denis's death, Reid's pattern of revolt from established religion to the discovery of nature structures the literal and symbolic meaning of this novel. After Denis refuses to attend church, nature with its seeming peace and harmony becomes his refuge. The sky is the symbol of a "great immensity," and the country of the gods is untroubled by care and sorrow. In moods of alienation and isolation, Denis believes himself to be different from everyone in his world. Feelings of being unwanted become assurances of exclusion from love as fictionalized in romances; he was certain that such love would never include him. In his desperate loneliness, he retreats to a pool near an old hawthorne tree where a ruin of a druidical altar with "its faint and faded stain of blood" echoes hauntings from the past of blood and sacrifice that recall Irish Hallowe'en as the Feast of the Moon.

Denis feels both attraction and repulsion for the pool, as the death wish begins in the voice calling, "Follow, follow, follow the wind and the water"; and the call continues in the hallucination of a naked figure playing a flute "on the other side of the stream" (89). Driven by forces outside himself, Denis chases the image through the undergrowth to the pool in which he sees his own face, "white, strange, half unknown" (90). Although Rusk discovers his pupil's nocturnal wanderings and knows of his nightmares, he is incapable of recognizing the seriousness of Denis's disturbance. Because Denis is unable to distinguish between superstition and reality, he thrusts against periodic darkness by enacting a ritual sacrifice to the moon whom, as high priest, he worships.

Even when the ritual becomes blood sacrifice, Rusk fails to grasp the boy's psychosis. Only when he sees the ceremony in which Denis burned incense, offered almond cakes, and drank libations to the moon goddess does he realize that Denis was not "playing a game" (160–61). Because Rusk's perception is not equal to the problem, he attributes the performance to an overactive imagination and to extreme sensitivity. When Rusk leaves the Bracknel house, and shatters former plans for travel abroad, Denis's world collapses. The impersonality of earth, water, and sky is no comfort against the "well of loneliness" that impels him to take his own life. Ironically, the reader sees that Rusk goes on to life believing in unseen forces controlling destiny and in the spirit informing all things; but some human dimension is lacking in his vision.

Within the tragedy of Denis's life and death, his obsession with the forces of materialism and evil destroying spiritual values is the price innocence pays for precocity. The miasma of evil that he keenly feels but insufficiently understands is experienced in a nightmare in which he watches his father struggling with a malignant form that overpowers him. In a ritual act, the nightmare repeats the murder to the former owner of the Bracknel house and foreshadows Mr.

Bracknel's death, with Alfred standing by. To Denis, the same dark forces are also using him as an instrument of their violence. Since no sacrifice is sufficient to turn the tide of evil polluting the world, nor is there a savior (Rusk) adequate to the task, Denis's despair results in suicide.

The *Bracknels* is a psychological study of disturbed adolescence in a world in which adult perceptions of reality leave much to be desired. Not even the educated tutor is sufficiently prepared to help Denis as he grows to sexual awareness with no knowledge about sexual instincts. To keep sex "out there," he is Endymion in love with the moon; by distancing the feminine, he can seemingly control natural forces. Since his friendship for Rusk is the deepest human relationship experienced, Denis desires no other nor does it come within his range. Although Rusk sees himself as the boy's protector, he fails to see that sensuality is no less basic to development than the "higher imagination." The dream world to which he retreats—one in which he could feel at given moments "the softened glow of the flaming vision beyond"—is sadly inadequate to the problems of his distressed student (277). The friendship fails because "the friends are not equal . . . the younger friend is more imaginative, intelligent and sensitive."[18] The odds are uneven, since Rusk, too, is fighting against an "invisible enemy who watches and waits, and when the hour has come strikes."[19]

The Bracknels shows an advance in Reid's technique over his two earlier novels. In placing the moon story at the center of the narrative, a return to time past becomes the pattern of regression against current violence. By using the haunted, obsessed mind of Denis, whose perception of evil surpasses that of either his family or his tutor, Reid is able to explore the evil manifest in everyday society and in so-called ordinary homes. The business ethic of Mr. Bracknel—who measures value by capital gains; his extramarital affairs and illegitimate son; his indifference toward his wife; and his hostility toward his children and in particular toward Denis—is a microcosm of the macrocosmic evil that surrounds the boy. Since Alfred is made in his father's image, inherited values become a way of life in which Denis wants no part. Because Mr. Bracknel finances Denis's education, he threatens his young son by insisting on a business training that is foreign to the boy's temperament. On the other hand, Rusk, who is trained in traditional education (Classical), is inadequate to Denis's interest in comparative religions and folklore. Therefore, he is no help in an area in which Denis has considerable curiosity. By himself, Denis is unable to cope with the reading he absorbs uncritically, misunderstands, and translates to blood sacrifice in his effort to appease forces he is powerless to control. As symbolic act, the ritual of primitive sacrifice that moves forward in time to bloodlessness raises the question of the efficacy of any religious sacrifice, ancient or modern, to dispel current violence. Indeed, Reid seems to say that no sacrifice can atone for the guilt of the world symbolized in the violence of son to father and father to son, for the violence of systems to persons, and of persons to each other. Denis's death assumes, therefore, larger significance as he tries to expiate what he believes to be unmitigated guilt by refusing to live in a world of evil. His tragedy resonates throughout the book as Rusk's life does not; for, since Rusk has learned to avoid evil by living his life according to his interests, he guarantees his survival. For Denis, there is no compromise—and no retreat.

The Bracknels shows to a marked degree the influence of Henry James's *The Pupil* (1891). Through the eyes of Morgan Moreen and his tutor Pemberton, James portrays the materialism of the Moreen family as it clashes with the Humanistic world to which young Morgan belongs. When Mrs. Moreen offers to let Pemberton virtually adopt Morgan, she parallels Bracknel's contract with Rusk to take Denis abroad; and death claims the life of each youth.

The Bracknels was more readily accepted by the reading public than Reid's two earlier novels. The domestic tragedy of the Bracknel family, the personal tragedy of the young Denis, and the setting of the beautiful Lagan valley made this book more human than his earlier works. An anonymous reviewer, writing in the *Nation* (London) on December 9, 1911, says: "Mr. Forrest Reid's excellence lies in the spiritual integrity with which he observes, analyzes, and records the 'unpleasant characteristics' of his interesting and disconcerting family, the Bracknels. . . . It would be a mistake to exaggerate the author's achievement, but we have selected it as a good example of a sombre work of art, which braces and fortifies the spiritual life by its very refusal to ignore things 'unpleasant.' "[20] *The Bracknels* launched Reid upon a successful literary career and pointed in the direction of both the Greek world and the region of the supernatural.

Reid spent the last year of his life rewriting *The Bracknels*, which was published posthumously under the title *Denis Bracknel* in

1947.[21] He did so because he wanted to bring the novel "into tune with *Apostate*,"[22] in which his dedication to Greece and the Greek world was explicit. Had he lived longer, he would have fulfilled his intention of rewriting earlier novels for the same reason. In a prefatory note to *Denis Bracknel*, Reid writes that this novel "is more than a revision. The theme remains, but from first to last it has been so completely rewritten that the result is practically a new book"(7). Stylistically, this assertion is true because of the greater directness and simplicity, and a stronger focus on the main problem of *Denis Bracknel*.

As in the original story, Denis's identity as a moon-worshipper is directed and sustained throughout the story. Although Basil de Selincourt regarded this aspect of the novel as a "luxury of the imagination," it is integral to the story's total meaning.[23] In *Denis Bracknel*, the moon story seems to dominate and control the emotion of the novel; and the family chronicle merely seems to provide the framework for Reid's idea. The family represents the antipathetic surroundings into which the sensitive Denis is cast and against which he rebels. The reader is prepared step by step in the revised novel for Denis's death, whereas his end in the earlier novel came somewhat, though not altogether, unexpectedly. At his publisher's insistence, Reid wrote a final scene for *The Bracknels* in which Rusk returns to say goodbye to the family before leaving for Australia. When he came to rewrite the story as *Denis Bracknel*, he restored the original ending, with the suicide of Denis and the discovery of his body by Rusk and Dr. Birch. The final question, "How are we to tell his mother?", adds poignancy to the story and was the kind of ending that Reid liked best. In addition, the failure of Rusk to understand Denis's adolescent disturbance seems to come out more directly in the later story. The background of nature in *Denis Bracknel* is the same as in *The Bracknels;* for to Reid, "the lovely Lagan valley, the river itself, the house, the woods—all these, I think *must* be there, *must* come through; for they had been my world from childhood, and were the kind of thing I found easiest to do."[24]

The Bracknels was the first fruit of Reid's maturity; it shows his continued interest in Greek material. When he rewrote this novel as *Denis Bracknel* in 1947, the Greek world had long since become an organic part of his vision.

IV   Following Darkness *and* Peter Waring

Because Reid was convinced that "the years of boyhood and adolescence are the most significant" and formative years in life, he again chose a boy hero for his next novel, *Following Darkness* (1912), which was later rewritten as *Peter Waring* (1937).[25] Dedicated to E. M. Forster, whom he had recently met, the 1912 novel is a psychological study of adolescence that Reid claimed was "the first novel of its kind to be written in English." The physical setting is the beautiful countryside of Northern Ireland—Newcastle Beach, the Mourne Mountains, and the green-hilled district of Derryaghy; but the psychic or supernatural setting, which extends "into the eighth sphere," accounts for the difference between *Following Darkness* and Compton Mackenzie's *Sinister Street* with which it is compared.[26]

Puck's song in Shakespeare's *Midsummer-Night's Dream* is the source of Reid's title, which suggests a mystery informing the story:

> And we fairies, that do run
>   By the triple Hecate's team,
> From the presence of the sun,
>   Following darkness like a dream. . . .[27]

The theme of the beautiful vision that is lost in Shelley's "Alastor" supports Reid's use of the Romantic quest to portray the childhood and adolescence of his hero, Peter Waring:

> Lost, lost, forever lost
> In the wide pathless desert of dim sleep
> That beautiful shape.[28]

The Preface to *Following Darkness* establishes the background of Peter Waring's life from fragments of an autobiography that have come into the possession of his friend Owen Gill after Peter's mysterious death. At the time of his death, Peter was an art critic living in Italy, and a follower of Morelli, whose reputation rested on a study entitled *Drawings of Early Italian Masters.* From the unusual circumstances and the suddenness of Peter's death in September, 1911, Owen believes that he was murdered. Since his life contains a strange story, Owen is planning to write about Peter from his memories of their schooldays in Belfast.

Looking back on their early friendship, Owen remembers Peter as an exceptionally gifted, intelligent student with "fine tastes," whose "aesthetic sense" was "morbidly acute," making his way of looking at life unfortunate (3). In time, their friendship changed because Peter tired of Owen; and when Owen met Peter a year before his death, he appeared to be "haunted by some secret thought" from which it became evident that he had come under the influence of "strange and disreputable persons" who professed to experiment in "occult sciences, spiritualism and even magic" (4). Restless and dissatisfied with life as Owen sees him, he became driven, hunted, and haunted. Among the fragments and memoirs, a picture of Katherine Dale, Peter's childhood sweetheart whom he painted from memory, suggests to Owen that his friend was inspired by a lost love whose beauty he was never able to capture in painting. As Owen examines the picture, the candle is extinguished and leaves him with the feeling that some presence in the room had "blown it out" (7).

Peter Waring, hero and narrator of the story, is an only child, the son of an Irish schoolmaster in County Down. His mother left his pedantic father shortly after the child's birth. Mrs. Carroll, a wealthy benefactor with a beautiful home in Derryaghy, virtually adopts Peter, opens her home to him, pays his expenses, buys his clothes, and intends eventually to send him to the university. At the opening of the story Peter is a dreamy, sensitive, and imaginative child. During the summer holidays, Gerald and Katherine Dale, Mrs. Carroll's twin nephew and niece, respectively, visit their aunt. When he meets Katherine, Peter falls in love at first sight. She is the embodiment of his dreams, colored by his reading Rhoda Broughton's novels and Shakespeare's *Venus and Adonis*. From an old picture of Prudence Carroll, an ancestor of Mrs. Carroll, Peter evolves a vision of ideal love and beauty that he soon attaches to the unimaginative, matter-of-fact Katherine. Actually, Peter has more in common with Gerald since both are lovers of music and art, but no friendship develops because Gerald's superior airs antagonize Peter.

After the summer vacation, the Dales leave Derryaghy; Peter is sent to a boys' school in Belfast; and he is obliged to board with relatives who live in a dreary flat in a shabby neighborhood. His painful experiences with his cousin George, who hoards nude photographs; his friendship with Owen Gill; his eventual discovery that Katherine can never love him; and his morbid despair and final decision to travel with Mrs. Carroll form the main incidents of the story.

Following Darkness is a portrait of the artist as a young man who is haunted by a beautiful painting of Prudence Carroll whose beauty cannot be matched in life nor equaled in art. The portrait then becomes the controlling image as the center from which action emanates and to which it returns, and raises at least two questions that the novel suggests but does not answer. Can Peter ever love a woman if the image of Prudence Carroll constantly gets in his way? If Peter is destined never to find meaning in sex or in religion, can he find himself through art? The memoirs reveal a frustrated artist whose unrealized potential is comprised of the art criticism by which he earns a living. Seemingly, the price paid for prostitution of his talents is death. What he intended to do, what he aspired to be, is the destiny of the unfulfilled. Had he lived, he planned to write an autobiography of his early youth in Ireland to capture the spirit of youth in words that Rembrandt had painted in lights and shadows. "Vague half realized yearnings" after an ideal in a "melancholy, dreamy passionate self" is the subject of this exceptional novel, as Reid fulfills the promise that Peter could not keep (10). In this novel, Reid celebrates youth as a passionate search for beauty; and the experiential morbidity that the character's later life reveals has its roots in childhood and in adolescence.

Following Darkness is a psychological study of a sensitive adolescent's growth through first love to a deeper understanding of himself. Katherine Dale, Owen Gill, and his cousin George McAllister are the characters through whom he is initiated into life. The conflict between father and son, whose temperamental and religious differences bring a parting of the ways, is sensitively portrayed from boyhood through adolescence in a series of encounters. Within three settings that correspond to social classes, houses become symbols of an economic scale that conditions the youth's possibilities; and his style of life reflects his quality of mind. A boy's own house may not be a home; certainly Peter's was not. His father's house is without humor; therefore, without grace. When Peter visits the wealthy Mrs. Carroll and is virtually adopted by her, Derraghy becomes home; and home is a garden. The garret room in the McAllister flat in Belfast repeats on a lower socioeconomic scale the inequalities in the system, as Reid realistically portrays Peter's repugnance to mediocrity, shabby materialism, and parochialism. On vacations, he returns to his father's house reluctantly, and spends most of his time with the Carrolls, who really become his family.

In structure, *Following Darkness* follows a traditional pattern of revolt and discovery that is common to novels of adolescence from Samuel Butler's *The Way of All Flesh* (1903) to the present.[29] Yet it has a unique lyrical quality that clearly marks its distance from Somerset Maugham's *Of Human Bondage* or several others cited in William York Tindall's excellent discussion of this genre.[30] Although Reid wrote *Following Darkness* four years before Joyce's *A Portrait of the Artist as a Young Man* (1916), a textual comparison of both novels reveals correspondences in imagery and in incident that is somewhat amazing.[31] Because *Following Darkness* is the objective correlative of *Apostate*, to which Reid added a romance, there is a noticeable repetition of episode and incident. To avoid duplication, the following analysis will highlight only those actions that form the substance of the novel. In so doing, however, the lyrical quality of the work is lost, Reid's superb use of animism is minimized, and the true voice of feeling is diluted.

In *Following Darkness*, as Peter looks back to his earliest memories, Reid selects those facets of experience that portray in a preschool boy the dawn of sex instincts that determine the characteristics of the adolescent. The feeling of a new suit of clothes, his love of animals, and his fondness for sentimental music, associated with a mother only vaguely remembered, set the pattern of revolt against his father and religion that is sensitively dramatized in a world of social inequalities. The exterior action moves between two houses that function as the symbols of two worlds: Peter's home is always life-denying; the Carroll residence, life-expanding. The exterior and interior world of house and home reflects the outer and inner tension by repetition in dreams of repulsion and desire, a dichotomy that carries throughout the novel. Whether daydreams take shape as an Arabian Nights landscape of pleasure, magicians, sphinxes, and gardens, or as the preferable private world of the Elysian Fields with an imaginary playmate, they repeat a symptom of discontent with the wasteland of unimaginative living and with a condition of intolerable loneliness.

Night dreams release sexual preoccupations and fear as the dreamer descends to "a charnel house or unknown place of death" (19) with his boy companion. If the descent evokes memories of past experience, the ascent reveals a horror of discovery by a god who is "all seeing,"—a revelation that in time necessitates rejecting compulsory religion. When Peter's break with formal religion comes (though its antecedents are rooted in childhood), sickness and convalescence herald a conversion to nature, as they commonly do in Reid's novels of adolescence.[32] The ecstatic discovery of nature, like a paean to earth, finds the dreamer linked in the chain of being with grass, plants, soil, and trees. Like a lover fumbling at the door of an echanted garden, he embraces the earth, making it obedient to "some obscure promptings of my body" (78). Feeling strangely fulfilled, purified, and peaceful, Peter lies half naked in the moonlight and imagines himself to be Endymion, and Katherine, the moon. A parallel incident occurs in Thomas Mann's *Joseph and His Brothers* as Joseph sits by the wall enjoying the light of the moon on his disrobed body.[33] When Peter leaves home for school in Belfast, his initiation into the public world begins as he struggles to keep his love for Katherine pure.

As John Milton states and as Reid implies, the "mind . . . can make a Heav'n of Hell, a Hell of Heav'n."[34] Pornographic photographs of nude women pollute the garret room in which Peter is trapped with his cousin George. From this inferno, Peter has no escape until he strikes up a friendship with Owen Gill, who willingly shares his interest about ideas of immortality, conversion, or the existence of God. Leo Tolstoi's theories on art and religion are daily conversation; in fact, the Russian novelist even answers a letter from Owen, who has come under the influence of the master. In several dramatic scenes, Peter, the agnostic, refutes Owen, the skeptic, in ironic dialectic; but Peter is always happy about this world of ideas that is explored with Owen.

At home in Derryaghy on Christmas Eve, Peter's loneliness returns with greater intensity, leading to thoughts of death as a release from unhappiness. As he walks across the golf course with Remus, his dog, the solitary wanderer across the sands of time is outlined against the sky. When nightmare recurs to torment the sleeper, religious anxieties house a dream wherein Peter rejects Christ, is stripped naked, is anointed by a dark angel, and is cast into the depths of hell. Compulsively driven by a need to confess, he visits a Roman Catholic church but is repelled by the expression of "invulnerable stupidity" in the eyes of a priest (222). Since he no more believed in free will than did his "Arabian Nights heroes," Peter has no sin to confess and no need of confessionals. In fact, religions are myths, as Owen explains; and Herbert Spencer's *First Principles* soon quells all his doubts. Although Peter knows by now that a man who believes in Pan can live "just as much for his soul as a Christian" (216–17), Owen concisely demolishes the Pan myth. Nevertheless, obsessed as Peter is by sin, he is certain that for him confession is wrong.

During the summer vacation, Peter's love for Katherine increases as his preoccupation with religion deepens. In his fear of growing up, he would like to keep the world the way it was in "old romances and fairy tales" (245). But life will not be stayed, and his love changes when he soon discovers that Katherine is not and never will be Prudence, a fact Peter feels deeply when he tries to make love to her. In one epiphany of many, Reid captures the rebuff in all its poignancy by centering his focus on Peter's getting up from the grass:

When I got up she was out of sight. I did not know how long I had lain there, but I made no attempt to follow her. As I brushed mechanically the earth and bits of grass and twigs from my clothes, I felt almost dazed. It had all passed, and I did not want to think. I heard the drowsy prattle of a stream, and became aware that I was hot and thirsty. I went down to it and followed the bank till I reached a deep green pool, from which, lying flat on my belly, I drank greedily. As I raised my head I saw my own image in the water—my bright eyes, my dark, flushed face, my coarse, ruffled hair. (282)

Peter's failure to win Katherine's love, his realization of his awkwardness as a lover, and his desire to die are delicately interwoven at the end of the story, which ends with Mrs. Carroll's making plans to take him abroad.

Both Owen and Peter serve as models for Reid to portray the consequences of a morbid esthetic sense in the development of an artist if he projects the adolescent into the future. In one way, Reid is both Owen and Peter, the Platonist and the esthete; and the struggle for integration is to reconcile opposites in order to relate to the world and to survive in it. Owen is not so fully developed as Peter is, yet there is a suggestion that he sees clearly, or that he has at least found a way to come to terms with life by keeping his ideals and by working through them to balance and sanity.

Through Reid's characterization of Peter, Reid uses double perspective to maximum capacity. As the reader is swept along by Peter's conflict with his father, his environment, his upbringing, and his religion, the world is seen through Peter's eyes and his reactions. Since he is caught in his dreams and lives by them, he cannot see what the reader sees as his intolerance of persons who are average, mediocre, ugly, deformed, or in any way unusual. His hostility toward his father becomes hate which is based on his intolerance of religious views that differ from his own. From this point forward, Peter's intolerance eats away his perspective; and his father's mannerisms—such as snuffling, shifting papers as he corrects student themes, using "thees" and "thous" when he prays, and shutting off lights to save money—inflame the fire of Peter's wrath. Peter lacks sympathy because he lacks heart.

Just as Peter found it difficult to say goodnight to his father, he fails to communicate with Katherine without being openly hostile to almost anything she says when she speaks about her travels in Switzerland or her visits to picture galleries. When she uses the inappropriate word "pretty," it sends him into a rage. His attitude toward Gerald is equally antagonistic, making communication virtually impossible. But Peter's intolerance is not limited to words: he is both cruel and violent to the village idiot whose "deformed face" and "slobbering mouth" so infuriate him that he strikes him with a stick (43). To Peter, the idiot has no right to intrude on the beautiful world of nature.

Several other incidents reveal Peter's insensitivity to the rights of others. He sees the scrub woman Margaret Beattie, who is deaf, as "an old witch who would ride away on her broomstick" (83). When an odd-looking man comes upon Peter and Katherine suddenly and stops to stare, Peter thinks that his fixed gaze is first "cruel," and then becomes corrupt; and Peter picks up a stone to harm him (69–70). At the McAllisters', he hates the whole atmosphere of "anxiety, worry and struggle" (138–39); and, since they live under impoverished conditions, the reader doubts that they enjoy a situation that they are helpless to change.

For the artist to see life clearly and to live it passionately, Reid seems to say, he must come to terms with the unfortunates of society, whether it be the idiot, the charwoman, or the headmaster whose body reeks with the odor of death. From this confrontation Peter all too easily flees, demanding that life give him only the refinements of civilization. Since he cannot come to terms with existential reality, art becomes an escape from flux, turmoil, and social misery. The irony deeply imbedded in the narrative is related to Peter's identity with nature, which, by the premise of his own theory, embraces all members in a single community. Since neither in childhood nor in adolescence can he embrace the alienated, the misfortunate, the ostracized, and the underprivileged, his pursuit of an ideal carries him beyond human limits and ultimately to death as we move back to the Preface. If his death is tragic, it is the tragedy of an esthete who has failed to find in life the vision he discovered in art. We may well raise the question whether his death is tragic at all, since tragedy implies transcendence, which Peter unfortunately lacks.

Reid's *Following Darkness* met with a mixed reception from the critics, but it failed almost completely with the reading public. Professor G. Stanley Hall, however, one of the foremost American authorities on adolescence, sent to Reid a most enthusiastic letter about the book. "It seems to me," he wrote, "the best presentation of the psychical phenomena of the adolescent ferment that I have ever seen. I shall take the liberty, unless you object, of referring to it in a forthcoming edition of my book on Adolescence."[35] Hall also suggested that Reid should write a book about the adolescent turmoil in girls; but Reid did not take kindly to this suggestion because he knew nothing about the subject. Moreover, he was not looking for a scientific reading public but for one that would appreciate his work as literature. He said of himself that he had "limitations—limitations of imagination, limitations of Sympathy"—and that he could never "even attempt to write a *Tess* or a *Madame Bovary*—let alone a book about adolescent girls"; and, of course, he was right.[36]

The most negative criticism of *Following Darkness* came from Miss Anne Macdonnell, a fellow reviewer on *The Manchester Guardian* who wrote that the novel could only appeal to "doctors and schoolmasters." She went one step further and asked: "It had some of the features of *Sinister Street*, hadn't it? Both seem to waste a good deal of talent on what is not very important. I am willing to face evil, even sordid evil, any amount of it, in the presentation of the drama of life, if it is the genuine thing. But a boy's little experiments in naughtiness, his imitative and furtive dashes into dark and vicious ways are by no means always the genuine thing. They are manifestations of his egoism and not at all interesting as a rule. Why flatter by elaborate analysis a boy's silly aping of better sinners than himself?"[37]

Both Edmund Gosse and Walter de la Mare encouraged Reid to continue writing novels. According to Gosse, "the contemporary English novel didn't matter; it was negligible"; and, in any case, Reid had "nothing to do with it, *Following Darkness* being in the Russian tradition."[38] Walter de la Mare was always encouraging, for he believed that "the years of childhood were the most vital and that time consciousness could not be handled imaginatively by too many writers."[39] One anonymous reviewer who caught the quality of the novel wrote that, "once read, *Following Darkness* is not a book that will be easily forgotten, and that is becoming a rare tribute for a novel."[40]

When Reid rewrote *Following Darkness* twenty-five years later, and published it in 1937 under the title of *Peter Waring*,[41] he had traveled far toward artistic fulfillment in the intervening period. A study of the parallel texts reveals, as we shall see, the mastery in style and in technique that came to Reid through experience and conscious artistry. The title of the work was changed because the public had associated *Following Darkness* with the Bible, thus attributing to it "a moral significance alien to the more imaginative suggestion" that Reid had in mind (PW, 9). He also deleted the lines from "Alastor" and substituted for them Puck's song from *A Midsummer-Night's Dream*, which was the source for the title of the original.

Discarding the preface of Owen Gill that had created a mysterious background for Peter Waring's death, Reid opens the new novel with Peter as the narrator revisiting the home of Mrs. Carroll after a lapse of twenty years. In his childhood he had been happy here, and the house is haunted by memories; the ghost of the young Peter takes him back to his boyhood days. As Peter climbs the stairs, he looks at the portrait of Mazo's young "Philip," which replaces that of Prudence Carroll in *Following Darkness*. By sleeping in the same room he had occupied as a child, he dreams the same dream as formerly; and he decides to set down "simply and faithfully what that boyhood was" (PW, 13). This method is much more direct and

literary than Reid's earlier attempt to convey the relationship between a painting and his story. Furthermore, the statement that
Reid made directly about the spirit of youth in *Following Darkness*
(10), he now does not state but makes it become the informing spirit
of the whole novel.

A comparative study of several passages drawn from these two
novels reveals Reid's stylistic maturity. In *Following Darkness*, he
refers to the "dawn of obscure sex instincts" (11); in *Peter Waring*
this becomes the "dawn of sex consciousness" (15). His "impressions" of his mother (FD, 13) are now "a vague recollection of my
mother" (PW, 15). The passage about the imaginary playmate in
Following Darkness is completely deleted. Moreover, in *Peter Waring* he adds a description of Peter's father that explains him more
fully and that allows the reader to see him in another light: "He may
have been different before the tragic failure of his marriage had
disillusioned and embittered him. I suspect that he had passionately
loved my mother; but I suspect too, that it was with a gloomy and
jealous love, for he had a gloomy and jealous nature" (PW, 21).

In order to emphasize annoyance with the momentary conversion
to religious fear to which Peter had succumbed in *Following Darkness*, Reid has Peter add in the revised novel: "A few months later I
felt nothing but contempt for that brief conversion" (PW, 23). In
Peter Waring, Reid has Peter grappling with Herbert Spencer's
"Unknowables" to strengthen the idea of time in relationship to a
beginning and an end (PW, 27). In order to intensify Peter's nature,
Reid adds the word "sensual" (PW, 28) to the "egotistical, proud,
impatient and stubborn" of *Following Darkness* (267). In the earlier
novel, a letter which Peter received from his father is described as
"amazingly unintelligent" (FD, 36); it is changed in *Peter Waring* to
read "annoying and tactless" (PW, 40). To the passage in *Following
Darkness* (72) in which Peter speaks of the complex forces in nature
as corresponding to the adolescent awakening, he adds, "for what I
imagined to be new was really old—old as life itself" (PW, 87). In
the passage in *Following Darkness* that is a paean to primitive instinct
when the boy embraces the earth, Reid had used the phrase
"obscure prompting" (78), but in *Peter Waring* he inserts the adjec-
tive "physical" to control his meaning: "The earth beneath me was
living and breathing, and obedient to some obscure physical
prompting . . ." (PW, 93).

When Owen and Peter discuss attendance at church, Owen says

in *Following Darkness,* "You'd like your children to give up going to church then?" (140). In *Peter Waring,* this statement becomes: "You'd like them to grow up godless atheists and idolators"? (164). George has a "licentious imagination" in *Following Darkness* (148), but this characteristic in the later novel becomes "a naturally las-civious mind" (PW, 174). Peter's reading in Herbert Spencer's *First Principles* in *Following Darkness* (217) is changed to Edward Caird's *Evolution of Religion* in *Peter Waring* (249). In order to stress Reid's concept of primitive time in contrast to clock time, he adds the following passage in *Peter Waring:* "and still I stood there, for the will to act was gone. . . . Myself motionless and detached, I had the strange impression of watching those others gliding steadily on and on in time. It was not an abstract idea, a metaphysical figure of speech: I seemed literally to see it—as if they were moving away from me in time that had become also space—moving away, never to return. Then with a startling distinctness I heard the clock strike ten" (PW, 346–47).

By the time Reid had recreated the character of Peter Waring, his earlier stylistic models had been outgrown. He came to realize through his discovery of clarity and directness in the writing of Anatole France that his own private spiritual vision demanded a "more naked and Grecian" style. In this later novel, Reid portrayed the disturbing childhood and painful adolescence of Peter with greater intensity; his method is more direct and objective; and his style is characterized by simplicity and quietness.

Two reviews may serve to point up the difference between *Following Darkness* and *Peter Waring.* Of *Following Darkness* an anonymous reviewer wrote: "In the depths of his consciousness Peter knows that he is 'following darkness.' It is so we read the book; but it is not so filled out and finished that it is readily discoverable. The music was bound to be incomplete; but the execution need not have been. The touch is not sure, especially in the latter stages of the book."[42] Years later, another anonymous reviewer of *Peter Waring* noted that: "There is no striving for effect, no touch of modernity in manner, style, or treatment, but a delicacy and grave beauty which have their own quiet appeal."[43]

As these reviewers indicate, Reid had during a quarter of a century perfected his style by study and by practice. Reid's growth, maturity, technical dexterity, and firm touch are everywhere appar-ent in *Peter Waring;* and these developments make it not only a "thing of beauty" but a significant modern novel. However, we must also take into consideration the change in taste of the reading public during the interval between these two novels.

CHAPTER 4

I Too Was in Arcadia:
The Middle Period (1913–1922)

DURING the years of 1913–1922, which brought the Easter Rebellion (1916) and World War I, Reid's novels that were written for the general reading public met with mixed reception. From
The Gentle Lover (1913) through *Pender Among the Residents*
(1922), he continued to explore with considerable subtlety unusual
states of mind and feeling in adults as well as in children. Although
his mythopoeic imagination probed other dimensions of experience,
Reid's strength lay in his vision of reality portrayed through the eyes
of an imaginative boy caught in a world of conflicting values. Except
for *The Gentle Lover*, which is set on the continent, the lake country
of Ulster is evoked with lyrical beauty as he paints with an artist's
touch the landscape of a country in which he was deeply rooted. The
religious dimension, which is also ever present, is sometimes strident; other times, muted. In the tension between two worlds, the
ideal and the real, the countryside is just beyond cobblestone
streets and tenement houses, or the scene is set in Carrick-a-rede or
Ballycastle by the sea; but the ideal world, the only real one, is the
world of childhood memory, imagination, art, and nature. Such a
world has a Wordsworthian starting point from which the journey is
made and to which the traveler returns; and the journey is always
home.

I The Gentle Lover

Hopeful of reaching a wider reading audience than formerly, Reid
wrote *The Gentle Lover: A Comedy of Middle Age* (1913) to please
public taste.[1] Planned as an "amour de voyage" in the manner of
Henry James, the novel is a fictionalized version of its author's
travels and observations in Belgium, France, and Italy. In this novel
Bennet Allingham, an uprooted Irishman from Ballinderry, returns
to Europe from America to seek a new lease on life. Like Winter-

83

bourne in James's *Daisy Miller*, he is a lonely, middle-aged bachelor
with unfulfilled childhood ambitions of becoming a painter. Brought
up in Ulster as a Presbyterian, he left the institutional church because he found in Humanism a noncreedal religion that was a more
genuine answer to life's complexities. In and through imaginative
paintings, largely on Greek themes, he discovers a spiritual dimension lacking in organized religion. Through Allingham as the central
intelligence who confronts varieties of religious experience, historical and modern, the conflict between religious persuasions is portrayed. On a personal level, his love and loss of Sylvie Grimshaw to
the young clergyman, the Reverend Mr. Halvard, and his subsequent marriage to Sophie Kilronan, is the slight plot on which the
story is built.

Allingham's rebirth begins on the Béguinage in Bruges when he
sees a red-haired Irish boy, Brian Grimshaw, the spirit of eternal
youth, strangely enough from Ballinderry. Through Brian, Allingham meets the Grimshaw family; the motley group who share his
pension; the clergyman Halvard who becomes his rival and adver-
sary; Miss Sophie Kilronan, his childhood sweetheart; and Brian's
sister Sylvie Grimshaw, whose beauty can only be compared to
famous paintings. Through his friendship for Brian and his love for
Sylvie, Allingham awakens to life and becomes its participant rather
than its spectator. Although his friends are Roman Catholic, religion
is no barrier to their relationship or to his subsequent marriage to
Sophie Kilronan after losing Sylvie Grimshaw to the young clergyman.

Few modern writers paint pictures that can compare with Reid's
sense of the place and the timelessness of Bruges except perhaps
Georges Rodenbach in his novel, *Bruges-la Morte*.[2] A primitive
religious spirit rests beneath the Medieval exterior of this "sad
Northern Venice" of old cathedrals, canals, and bridges that is an
oasis in the desert of modern civilization.[3] A city with "a distinct
personality," Bruges corresponds to a traveler's need for "joy, love,
sorrow or renunciation."[4] To Reid and to Rodenbach, each town or
city represents "a condition of soul that unconsciously enters into
our life, a fluid that emanates imperceptively into atmosphere."[5] In
1915, Reid recalls Bruges as the most excellent survival of Medieval
Europe, momentarily saved from the bombs and shells of World
War I, though less prosperous since the collapse of the Hanseatic
League.[6] Reid captures the old city in a mood of haunting melan-

choly as he paints in autumnal tones the spell of witchcraft by night. Against this background, he portrays Allingham's rebirth of feeling through his relationship with Brian and Sylvie Grimshaw.

Sienna, the city of the sun, Reid outlines against a sky of burnished gold sleeping in a tranquil dream of the Middle Ages. Allingham's journey is like a tour through art history with Walter Pater, Bernard Berenson, and Grant Allen who are also guides to the imaginative life (138). Each city in turn reveals a different aspect of Allingham's loneliness as he gradually moves to a deeper understanding of life through love. Recalling his first visit to Westminster Abbey, where choir boys from the cathedral school were more meaningful than the cathedral, he wonders whether the Ethiopian can change his skin or the leopard his spots. In Paris, a reverie reveals his desire to have a son; and, as his journey progresses, Brian and Sylvie become his dream children. In Pisa, where the tower is the symbol of eternity, he lectures to the Reverend Mr. Halvard about married love as the highest love for sensible living. In Florence, Botticelli's "Birth of Venus" advances the subtle love theme which is completed by the tour's end; for Allingham's future returns him to Northern Ireland married to Sophie Kilronan.

To the sense of the place as the magic by which Allingham is reborn, the myth of the Golden Ass from Apuleius advances the metamorphosis theme. Bruges becomes by moonlight the witch-haunted island of Thessaly, a geography symbolic of perfection in life reflected and captured through imaginative paintings on mythology. As Allingham guides the Grimshaws through museums and churches, his comments reveal his esthetic paganism; and Reid explores within this framework the conflict between Humanism and Christianity. Although Allingham found in Humanism a dimension of spirituality lacking in orthodox religions and in "spurious" spiritual societies, his irritability with Christian belief suggests a lack of integration in his personality. Because his spiritual odyssey also lacks the compassion that obtains in George Eliot's portrayal of religious conflict, his journey is a circular rather than a mind-expanding one. In a conversation with Sylvie, who questions his personal beliefs, his answer reveals his aristocratic bias as he declares that he believes "in making the most of this present life, living with the best people, in the pleasantest surroundings." He continues: "I am not fond of walking through the slums . . . nor do I find so much charm in the unfortunate and uneducated as in the

fortunate and the cultivated." When she suggests that duty requires
one to help the unfortunate, he "marvels at the magic of youth
which could cast a glamour over the dullest platitudes" (162). Although he successfully smashes idols as he sees them by unmasking
in turn the so-called "illusions" of Roman Catholicism, Epis-
copalianism, and Spiritualism, his arguments are often trite, his
tone strident, and his "militant skepticism," which he disclaims, is
only another mask for his prejudices (162).

In a series of dramatic scenes, the conflict between Humanism
and Christian values begins, grows, and is resolved to Allingham's
satisfaction. When the carillons sound canonical hours in Bruges, he
is attracted by the music but repelled by the imposition of liturgical
time on nature's time. From this moment, his early hostility toward
Roman Catholicism returns with all its old intensity; and his hostile
attitude grows as his eye focuses on realistic paintings of ungainly
Madonnas in wall niches and on a statue of a crucified Christ with a
"white drawn face" and blood-streaked body. His hostility reaches
its climax when a religious processional comes into view and when
his aversion centers on the new curé, "fat, bald, with shifty eyes,
loose thin mouth, an almost simian absence of forehead"; but Allingham tells Brian that the priest may be a good man even though a
Roman Catholic (80). When altar boys dressed as young John the
Baptists appear bearing a cross, he considers them "lithe, brown-
skinned fauns, . . . a survival from the antique past" (78).

Allingham's next quarrel is with Spiritualism, and it is portrayed
when the Reverend Mr. Halvard, a newly ordained minister in the
Anglican Church, takes him on a visit to the famous Flamel, a
Spiritualist who professes psychical powers of communication with
the spirit world. The ostensible purpose of the visit represents a
joint search for a spiritual reality that counteracts materialism, but
the description of the séance is the means by which Allingham both
unmasks and parodies the "fraudulency" of Spiritualism in its claims
to contact souls who have passed to the other world. Even though
he believed in hallucinations, he did not believe in ghosts.

When Allingham discusses religious questions with the Anglican
priest, his quarrel with institutional religion brings Anglicanism
under scrutiny. The minister's idealism and immaturity are pitted
against the agnosticism of Allingham as both continue to search for
spiritual meaning. From the middle of the novel to its conclusion,
Allingham relentlessly pursues Halvard, the clergyman, who has

fallen in love with Sylvie Grimshaw. Caught in the demands of celibacy, Halvard flees to Pisa; and Allingham follows him. In a scene of dramatic confrontation, Allingham unleashes a tirade about celibacy as unnatural, abnormal, and unhealthy. Against the force of this argument, the clergyman's defense of celibacy by mouthing a story of St. Catherine of Sienna whose only food was the consecrated host, is the thrust that serves Reid's narrative purpose of de-mythologizing religious beliefs. Allingham's success in the first round leads to his debunking the literature of the saints as stories "reeking of the hospital and the charnel house" (195). In short order, he reaches the end from which he began. "Religion," he says, may throw "a deceptive glamour over the unnatural, but it can never be made natural." For mental health, "a day out in the woods, or by the sea is a better tonic for the soul than incense, a plunge in the river than half an hour in the confessional" (195). Since the argument from nature convinces Halvard that his love for Sylvie has priority over priestly orders, he returns from Pisa to make his future marital plans known. Three months later, Allingham and Sophie Kilronan also decide to marry. Religious beliefs and differences are no barrier to their future together.

Within the overarching conflict between Humanism and Christian orthodoxy, Reid uses Allingham's tastes for Italian Renaissance paintings on Greek themes in preference to most Medieval art to reenforce the importance of the Greek ideal and to deepen the texture of his work. Since naturalness and beauty as the sensuous embodiment of an ideal are among his criteria for great art, such works as those of Memlinc and Van Eyke in Bruges, Watteau's "Embarquement pour Cythère" at the Louvre, and Botticelli's "Birth of Venus" in the Uffizi Gallery in Florence function as touchstones for the art appreciation of the travelers. By comparison, Botticelli's "Annunciation" and other paintings on liturgical themes fail to approach the exquisite art of the antique and the "gold" of poetic landscapes. Haunted by memories of a magnificent past of which Greece is the symbol, Allingham yearns for an earthly paradise. In his reverie, Bruges elicits Thessaly, just as Paris recalls an unspecified Greek island; for, in each case, the pastoral is the ideal landscape as a retreat from the noise and commerce of cities.

In order to characterize the Reverend Mr. Halvard symbolically, Reid uses the Greek myth of Hippolytus from Pater's essay "Hippolytus Veiled."[7] Since Halvard is naive, he regards his relationship to Sylvie as a Platonic friendship; but she has fallen in love with him. When he gives her Pater's romance to read, she pictures Halvard as the youthful Greek hero with "golden hair . . . clear, delicate skin . . . finely moulded features, . . . beautiful forehead . . . and graceful form" (228). The likeness between Hippolytus and the young clergyman is even more complete in the light of the religious ideal to which he is dedicated, for she sees both the pagan Hippolytus and the Christian minister as symbols of the highest idealism—one based on "the power of renunciation, the renunciation of one's personal pleasures for the love of a spiritual beauty" (228). When Allingham unveils Hippolytus, however, she is prepared to accept Halvard's renunciation of his priestly vow of celibacy, which then frees him to marry her.

Reid was not happy about *The Gentle Lover* or about the character of Allingham, whom he later regarded as "not essential." To Reid, "the story, I felt, was just a little thin, needed an incident or two. To a realist it is a severe handicap to be by temperament romantic, unless, like Flaubert, he is sufficiently resolute to keep the two elements in his nature separate, and write alternate books in which, without confusing, he expresses both of them. I think I found the way eventually, but for a long time, and certainly in *The Gentle Lover*, I fumbled."[8]

The Gentle Lover was not well received by either the press or the public. In writing this novel, Reid apparently lost his hold on the mythical method of writing that had been most effective for conveying his meaning in his earlier works. Although he still maintained his sense of the past as living in the present, he was less successful in projecting his meaning through adult characters than through the mind of the adolescent. Although this novel shows an advance in Reid's use of dialogue and in the relationship of characters to one another and to society, Reid made a too conscious strain to achieve effectiveness in his attempt to prove by dialectic the superiority of Humanism over Christianity. The conflict is real enough, but it is stated rather than dramatized. Furthermore, though Reid is excellent in describing masculine types—Brian, the Reverend Mr. Halvard, Allingham, and even the repulsive Flamel—his Sylvie is so stereotyped and ideal that the reader feels that he drew her from a statue rather than from life. Miss Sophie Kilronan and Mrs. Grimshaw serve merely as background and are not fully developed characters.

Reid's descriptions of Bruges and Italy are poetic; he captures in words what a painter might arrest through light and shadow. His descriptions of Florence on the Arno River and of sleeping Sienna in the sun may stand comparison with those in Henry James's *Roderick Hudson* since both works are painted with sensitive, delicate strokes. Reid has the ability to evoke various moods and to relate the changing aspects of day and night to the interior state of his characters. The device of having Allingham travel from Bruges to Florence, Paris, Pisa, and back, coupled with day trips in and out of Florence, gives variety to the story and makes Allingham's quest for beauty and spiritual reality more convincing.

The Hellenic element in *The Gentle Lover* is not as pronounced as it was in the novels previously discussed, yet it is present as an undercurrent and an informing spirit. Bennet Allingham as drawn is a frustrated modern artist whose concept of beauty is based on a Greek esthetic. From Greek sculpture and literature he has learned that the only real beauty is spiritual. When he discovers this spirit in the youthful Sylvie and Brian Grimshaw, his attitude toward life changes and he becomes more human. Within the novel several Hellenic themes emerge: the friendship between Allingham and Brian; the ideal of beauty as embodied in the youth of Brian and Sylvie; the conflict of Humanism with established religions and asceticism; and the contrast between Medieval Bruges and the Thessaly of Apuleius as a study in moods. Because Hellenism is integral to Reid's philosophy of life and esthetics, it colors even a novel like *The Gentle Lover*, which was professedly designed as a departure from his usual adolescent subject and his "other landscape."

II   At the Door of the Gate

The following quotation, prefixed to the title page of *At the Door of the Gate* (1915), originally entitled *The Three Women* (which the author preferred), introduces the hound of heaven theme that permeates and controls the story: "Whither shall I go from Thy spirit? Or whither shall I flee from Thy presence? If I ascend up into heaven, Thou art there; if I make my bed in hell, behold, Thou art there. If I take the wings of the morning, and dwell in the uttermost parts of the sea; even there shall Thy hand lead me, and Thy right hand shall hold me."[9] On a biblical level of meaning, God pursues the soul who flees Him, just as the hound follows the hare in its chase. To this theme, Reid subtly couples the three Greek god-

desses of destiny, the Moerae, who parallel the three women in his
hero's life. In antiquity, the goddesses of destiny preordained the
course and outcome of each human life: Clotho spins the thread of
life, Lachesis determines its length, and Atropos cuts it off. These
goddesses are often revealed as cruel and jealous because they
thwart the desires and plans of men.

Although Reid maintains that this novel was a "solitary attempt to
write a purely objective and realistic novel about Belfast lower middle class life," his dedication to Walter de la Mare is a clear indica-
tion that the term "realistic" must be extended to include psychic
experience.[10] *At the Door of the Gate* is similar, therefore, in theme
to *The Gentle Lover* insofar as both involve a search for spiritual
reality by which to transcend everyday life. Both employ myth functionally: the myth of Hippolytus in *The Gentle Lover* and the myth
of Cain and Abel in the 1915 novel. By artistically manipulating the
mythical mode, this narrative becomes a study of multileveled reality.

The story begins in the lower middle class neighborhood of Myrtle Row at the end of Blenheim Gardens in Belfast. In the social
circle of Blenheim Gardens live the professional class of physicians,
lawyers, and professors, and Mrs. Wilberforce, whose constant discussions of the problems of the "working classes," their misplaced
ambitions, and the evils of a spreading democracy represent the
attitude of her upper middle class social milieu. Number Eight
Myrtle Row is the home of a widow, Mrs. Seawright, who is described in the words of Mrs. Wilberforce as "an admirable woman of
her class" (4). In order to support her family, Mrs. Seawright, a
working woman of lower socioeconomic status, manages a combina-
tion post office and lending library. Class distinctions are thus carefully and realistically established in the early stages of the story, in
which the two divisions of the neighborhood become symbols of
social divisions in Belfast society.

Each member of the Seawright family is as acutely portrayed as
the matriarchal system itself is. By means of a flashback, we learn
that Mr. Seawright was an attractive Irishman who seldom worked,
who drank heavily, and who died in time to avoid a scandal involving a misappropriation of company funds. Although his widow kept
the "futile, hopeless story" from the children, and professed no
more love for him in death than she had felt for him in life,
nevertheless her sole ambition was to set a headstone over his

grave. That he was "a poor specimen of humanity" in no way diminished the pleasure she derived in visualizing the erection of "something beautiful" in his memory, like a "marble angel with the broken harp" (31).

The contrast between the two Seawright sons, Martin and Richard, is striking. Martin, his mother's favorite, is a handsome boy with delicate features whose physical appearance conceals a weakness deeply rooted in a mother complex; and he is an excellent conversationalist with many social graces. Although he drinks heavily, gambles, and is naturally cruel, he brags that "no matter what else he had done, . . . he had always gone to church to please his mother" (80). Richard Seawright is pictured as a sensitive, imaginative, taciturn boy who wants to write poetry, but economic conditions demand that he leave school to enter the tea trade. The first half of the novel is concerned with the storm and stress of his adolescence; his resentment toward Martin, his mother's favorite; his antagonism toward his middle class environment; and his rebellion against religion. The second half tells the story of his marriage, disillusionment, and strange conversion.

Grace Mallow, the third member of the Seawright household, is the daughter of Henry Mallow, now deceased, whom Mrs. Seawright had once loved. Although an ugly birthmark disfigures her face, she is inwardly a sensitive, understanding, and artistic person. Through her music, she expresses the love for Richard that she has never dared to reveal. In time, music becomes her life, bringing her fame and recognition. Ultimately, she marries Mr. Campbell, an older man, only to discover that she is still in love with Richard.

The Cain and Abel myth, coupled with the Greek idea of fate or destiny, enables Reid to direct the story so that it works on several levels simultaneously. *At the Door of the Gate* is a powerful presentation of an artist's alienation from God who pursues the soul He has marked with the brand of Cain until an emotional crisis precipitates a conversion to nature. As a story of religious conversion, Reid's is similar to the experience of Mark Rutherford's discovery of Wordsworth's *Lyrical Ballads* after he had been emancipated from Calvinism.[11]

The early action of the story portrays the tension between Richard and Martin (Cain and Abel), which is based upon temperamental differences and upon Richard's growing envy of Martin's place in his mother's affections. When Richard is forced to enter the tea trade,

his jealousy deepens and intensifies; and, because the commercialism of his job conflicts with the idealism of his private world, he
withdraws further from reality. His tragedy, if we may call it such, is
that of an idealist caught in a middle class world of values alien to his
nature. When he meets Rose Jackson, whom he sees as a symbol of
"wronged innocence," she tricks him into marriage after a weekend
in the country. Their tumultuous relationship deteriorates until
their son is born, for Rose is having an affair with Martin. When
their son dies, with Martin implicated in his death, Rose commits
suicide; and Richard, in a fist fight, accidentally knocks Martin over
a cliff. In his suffering, Richard prays to God for enlightenment
which comes at the height of a thunderstorm. In the rain, thunder,
and lightning, he experiences a mystical communion with the earth
and feels that he *has* seen God.

Reid uses the Cain and Abel myth, as well as Nemesis and Greek
imagery, to explore a family relationship in which Oedipal elements
foreshadow tragedy. From the opening of the story, Richard's exceptional qualities reveal him as an archetypal artist who outwardly
resembles "a youthful Greek divinity" (7); inwardly he bears the
brand of Cain that predestines him for tragedy. Just as Richard's
violence is foreshadowed in a dream in which he kills Martin and is
forever damned, his creativity is revealed in the poems he writes
about birds, trees, flowers, and clouds. Both as Cain and as Endymion, he is not only torn and divided by the demands of a business
world but also haunted by spiritual visions that he tries to re-create
in his writing. Socialism, Home Rule, women voters, or "marriage
and the value of the home" (100) have no place in his thoughts. In
his loneliness, he creates a dream companion who shares his ideas
and feelings; and as his adolescence yields to maturity, the image of
a "faun" becomes a "woodland god" to symbolize his entrance into
the adult world. In a scene in which he flees from a family picnic—
repulsed by liquor, noise, and community singing—a plunge into
cold water is his baptism into nature. Later, when he goes to the
university, he develops his interest in Greek culture, Classical literature, and Zeller's *Socrates and the Socratic Schools* (120); and he
finds in such studies confirmation of his own beliefs.

After Richard meets Rose, his unfortunate projection of ideal
beauty, known only through the Apollo Belvedere, results in increased dissatisfaction with the bonds that limit his passion for freedom. His fantasies house the "other landscape" where a tropical

sun, palm trees, and "the dusky skins of his own playmates" (141) explain his proclivities as they foreshadow the failure of his marriage. The use of Browning's "Porphyro's Lover," wherein the lover kills his beloved "to keep her pure . . . to save her from himself and from herself," structures his aversion to marriage and his unsuitability for it (196). In their premarital relations, Rose is a "convolvulus," partner to a hated intimacy (205); during the honeymoon, "there was something in their intimacy which . . . made him feel ashamed. He was caught in it, but he felt it like bird-lime clinging to the beating wings of his spirit. It was as if all his life long he had trembled in awe before some holy and mysterious shrine only to find, on drawing a curtain, no beautiful and divine figure, but a primitive image of wood or clay" (220). The asceticism of his nature, coupled with "other instincts . . . equally strong" (225), increased quarrels and erotic reconciliations that led to Rose's suicide.

The Cain motif repeats on a second level the violence of Richard to persons. After his quarrel of dramatic intensity that ends in Martin's death, the nightmare of his childhood becomes his adult reality. Although he sees himself as Jacob wrestling with the angel, beating "at the gate of the infinite," praying to know the "spiritual reality" behind things that are not the "mere invention of a few exalted minds," the reader sees his psychological problems more clearly (299–300). The rationalization of violence and the author's interpolations reveal a sympathy with the artist as a law unto himself whose freedom is destroyed by women. When he hears a voice in the wind saying that "as the heart panteth after the water brooks, so panteth my soul after Thee, O God" (315), his leap of faith demands considerable suspension of disbelief from the reader.

The final scene is a rhapsody to nature dramatized against the background of lightning, rain, and thunder wherein Richard is reborn. After his rebirth and after he has dropped down on the sodden grass, free from guilt, he has a sense of being "at one with Nature" as wave after wave flowed over him "in a great cleansing flood that sanctified and blessed" (316). His discovery of a religion in nature, animistic in kind and timeless, is portrayed as a mystical discovery of a vision of God (318). In his new-found freedom, he has "no ties, no one depending on me" (328). "I must be His," he expostulates, "so that He can claim my life or death at any moment" (328). It is Grace Mallow who gets to the heart of Richard's problem when she says: "It was your mother you loved best of all (if you ever loved anyone)—not Rose, not me" (331). The controlling myth of Cain by a process of transvaluation returns Richard, the hunted and the possessed, to God (seen here as the spirit of the earth), in keeping with God's original promise of protection even to those He has marked. Richard's final rejection of Grace is symbolic of his freedom from the "three women"—Rose, Grace, and his mother—who were the disruptive forces in his life. Once he has rejected them, he is free to wander like Cain wherever his own nature will take him.

An anonymous reviewer noted that Richard's unusual conversion demands of the reader "a special knowledge of Belfast psychology . . . to realize how in spite of the brand of Cain, Richard is able to attain the door which not only includes a disastrous past, but opens on a fair, if unspecified future."[12] Moreover, Basil de Selincourt was partially right in his attitude toward Reid's use of the supernatural. He believed that Reid depended too heavily on the "spiritualistic," the "magical," and "a kind of sixth sense" in "portraying his vision of the spiritual."[13] Reid defended his own position by stating that he was not really interested in the trappings of supernaturalism but in "an animistic conception of nature—something that the listening spirit hears in the sound of the waves, or feels in the silence of the woods—a telepathic communication from a spirit that seemed . . . both human and divine."[14] He compares his own state of mind and his underlying belief to Wordsworth's pantheism, which he felt was also a "psychic experience."[15]

At the Door of the Gate was the first of Reid's novels to be published in America; it was not very favorably received or understood. One critic, however, found it attractive "by reason of its unusual treatment of an unusual theme, the intrinsic interest of the story it tells, its vital and clear-cut characters, and the charm of its style." He admits, too, that he found it interesting because "of a certain cryptic and elusive significance which we feel we ought to have grasped, but cannot be quite sure of."[16]

Several British reviews sensed the particular quality of the novel. "Its origin," one reviewer noted, "is related to the spiritual chaos of our times, the tentative reaction from their grosser materialism, the inability of orthodox religions either to square man's dealings with his fellows . . . with God, or to offer any imaginative exposition of his transcendental destiny." Reid, he believed, was the only one of the contemporary novelists to attempt to come to terms with what may "happen to man in the next world" since man was "destroying

himself so thoroughly in the immediate world." The story, he de-
clared, "is strained" but "well conceived, and told with subtlety and
power."[17] The reviewer for the London *Times Literary Supplement*,
who paid tribute to Reid's ability to re-create Belfast and its society
in Realistic fashion, commented that "one admires the sustained
skill with which in a succession of small strokes Mr. Reid builds up
his admirable story."[18]

As a novel of religious experience that treats conversion to nature
as an answer to orthodox religion's failure to satisfy man's needs, the
change wrought in Richard through his discovery of nature, paral-
leling St. Paul's discovery of Christ, shows the influence of
Wordsworth's "apostasy" and Mark Rutherford's "conversion." In
each psychic change, a vital spirit of nature replaces "the old deity,
once alive, but gradually hardened into an idol."[19] As a novel written during World War I, it confronts violence and materialism by
structuring peace and freedom in a more desirable world. *At the
Door of the Gate* is the most subtle and complex novel that Reid had
written up to this time.

III The Spring Song

When Reid wrote *The Spring Song* (1916),[20] he hoped it might
"wake up the libraries" to include books that portrayed children as
they were, not as they ought to be.[21] Although he disliked maudlin
sentimentality, he believed a sentimental view to be valid if a writer
could convey a child's feeling of fellowship with birds and beasts
comparable to that found in the *Greek Anthology* and in pre-Socratic
and Socratic philosophy. On the title page of this novel the following
quotation from John Donne establishes the complexity of Reid's
thirteen year old hero Griffith Weston, whom he affectionately calls
Grif throughout the story: "I am a little world made cunningly/ Of
elements and an angelic sprite."[22] The opening chapter, introduced
by a quotation from Thomas Nashe, sets the tragic mood: "So fair a
summer, look for never more."[23] Subsequent chapters are introduced by verses from Renaissance and Romantic poets in order to
intensify the atmosphere.

The title, *The Spring Song*, taken from an Italian aria by Gian
Peruzzi, announces the flute song that is dominant from beginning
to end. By the use of antiphonal structure, Reid portrays Grif Weston's response to the music of a silver flute as it attracts yet disturbs
him. Thematically, Reid fuses the myth of Orpheus and Pan to move

the story along as he explores the psychologically disturbed mind of the highly imaginative Grif from summer to early autumn in the Ballinderry district of County Antrim. *The Spring Song* is a moving tale in which Reid sensitively portrays the story of five English children, the Westons, and their governess Miss Johnson, during one summer's vacation at their grandparents' house. The Glebe, in Ballyreagh, Ireland, while their parents travel abroad. Four of the Westons are sturdy, lively, normal adolescents and children, whereas the boy Grif is an exceptional and strange child. Although not "abnormal," he is surely very different by precocity and temperament, and his physical hold on life is slight.

The dominant story is devoted to Grif, although Reid skillfully portrays the activity of each character, their intrigues, their games, and their growing pains with a sense of simultaneity. Thus the ordinary contrasts sharply to the tensioned drama of Grif's mental anguish of which the others are completely unaware. Edward at fifteen, and Barbara at twelve years of age, evidence the self-consciousness that comes with adolescence as their preoccupation with their hair and clothes reveals their changing state. Of the younger children, "fat little Ann," who is ten, is always running and forever out of breath in her effort to keep up with Jim or Grif; while Jim, nine years old, hovering on the borderline between the "lively" and the "naughty," loves jokes, riddles, the circus, airplanes, and "wireless telepathy." Since Grif is too delicate to join in sports and has no inclination for them, he spends his time reading the *Arabian Nights*, taking nature walks, or listening to voices in the wind. Palmer Dorset, a schoolmate of Edward's, also joins the Westons who leave school before the semester's end because of an outbreak of diphtheria. Pouncer, the Weston's wonderful bulldog and Grif's constant companion, is a vital addition to this enlarged family. Grif's grandfather Canon Annesley, a folklorist who is writing a book on fairies, and Aunt Caroline, the practical homemaker, are homespun, warm characters. Captain Narcissus Batts and his sisters, Miss Jane and Miss Nancy, are as unusual as they are kind and hospitable despite the death of their young nephew Billy Batts Tremaine around whom their life was centered. The only dissonant note in an otherwise idyllic world is the eccentric organist, Mr. Clement Bradley, alias Tennant. Dr. O'Neill, the family physician, is a character almost as gullible as Palmer Dorset, yet not quite so callous.

By means of a story within a story, Reid portrays Grif's physical and mental breakdown by his contact with the eccentric, morbid, and unbalanced Bradley, whose horror tales bring Grif to the edge of a nervous breakdown and add to his physical illness. With heightened emotion and with graphic intensity, Bradley tells Grif that his former music pupil, Billy Tremaine, is trying to lure Grif to himself by the sound of the flute. Since Grif hears the flute both day and night, he is deluded into thinking that Billy is, in fact, trying to "get at him." Because the nature of Grif's illness puzzles everyone, Dr. O'Neill questions Palmer about Grif's activities. Since Palmer considers himself a detective, he tells Dr. O'Neill what he knows in fact and what he suspects about Bradley. Only too receptive to Palmer's theories, Dr. O'Neill and the amateur detective pay a visit to the organist. When thus confronted Bradley feels accused and trapped; his mental balance is so disturbed that he goes to the church at midnight, plays the organ at full stop, sets the church on fire, and hurls himself to death from a turret. Even after Bradley's death, since Grif's recuperation is far too slow, Dr. O'Neill counsels him to visit the Batts again in order to get a better perspective on the real Billy Tremaine. When Grif complies and tells Miss Nancy the stories that Bradley had told him about Billy, she sees the delusions for what they are, and the horror of them. In her compassion she shows Grif Billy's room with his books and toys intact. From her account Grif learns that Billy was a normal, fun-loving boy. With a feeling of great release and relief from the burden of horror he had borne so long, Grif sees the truth as it is and falls into a deep sleep in Miss Nancy's arms. Although Miss Nancy is convinced that Grif will recover, the second call to lunch fails to rouse him. Freed from this last nightmare of dread and delusion, Grif's final revelation in which he sees the truth clearly is insufficient for the shock his mind has suffered and he dies.

For his narrative purpose, which is to portray the impact of a deranged mind on that of an innocent, sensitive boy, Reid uses the structure of the archetypal perilous journey with its strange and unusual encounters as the thread of plot on which Grif's story moves in counterpoint to the normal rhythm of everyday life at The Glebe. If, on one hand, Grif's adventures partake of the magic of nature and bright dreams of a boy companion, they also plunge him into a world of the sinister, the macabre, and the ghastly. In narrating both Grif's physical and spiritual experiences, Reid uses images of light and darkness, dream and nightmare, to capture his hero's thoughts and feelings. For example, when Grif first visits the house and garden of Captain and Miss Nancy Batts, he felt as if this were "a dream place to which he was coming back." Although time ran out before he could see Billy Tremaine's room, Captain Batts showed him Billy's flute. Grif felt as if both the garden and the house were haunted, but not by "ghosts," because the peaceful atmosphere there was untouched by either melancholy or regret. That Grif is obsessed with "ghosts" is evident from his second encounter with the organist who is also preoccupied with them. Although Grif was at first fascinated by Bradley's queer clothes, his silvery hair, and his beady eyes, as Grif's uncertainty about him increases he feels haunted by something vague and sinister. To satisfy his curiosity, and unnoticed by Bradley, Grif slips into the church, climbs to the choir stall, and, while listening to the music, falls into a reverie that more closely resembles a nightmare. In Grif's transposed state, the organist is revealed in a procession of hooded men against the background of a church, a large crucifix, and a tower from which a huge black bird sweeps down on an old city. Suddenly the trance is broken and reality returns when Bradley screams at Grif for stealing upon him like a "ghost."

In another adventure Grif visits the cool, green churchyard in order to read the Apochryphal story of Tobias and the angel, only to discover Billy Tremaine's name inscribed on a tombstone. Before Grif has time to digest the fact of Billy's death, Bradley appears with a sinister warning about Billy trying to "get at" Grif by playing on the flute. The flute song, Bradley says, was the song sung by his pupil Billy Tremaine before he died. As Bradley is obsessed by the dead returning to possess the living, so Grif feels threatened by Bradley's stories, walks in his sleep, becomes ill, and is confined to his bed. From Bradley there appears no escape, since Grif must now submit to Bradley's visit and listen to even more sinister tales as oppressive as they are frightening. Not only does Bradley believe in ghosts, but he compounds Grif's fears by enumerating his own nightmares in which he is assaulted by a vampire, has murdered his brother, and has lost his shadow. By the end of Bradley's prolonged stay, Grif, in a state of delirium, is convinced that the organist's shadow is still in his room; that it has settled on him like a cold mist; and that it is still clutching at his throat in a stranglehold. When Grif is awakened by Pouncer jumping on his bed, he knows that Pouncer has saved him from the hideous monster and has chased the shadow away. At the end of the story, Palmer's use of the word "shadow" causes a panic in the organist's mind which culminates in his suicide. For Grif, however, although the spectre is removed by Miss Nancy's calm revelation of Billy Tremaine's normality, he, too, has answered the call of Orpheus.

On the surface, *The Spring Song* is a psychological study of hallucination and delusion in both child and adult; but at a deeper level, Reid explores psychic states of consciousness in Grif's response to nature as he feels "presences" in the wind or the spirit in trees. The murmur of the pines becomes "whispering voices" in which the "Spring Song" holds him captive. To portray both physiological and psychological changes in Grif's growth from childhood to adolescence, the "Spring Song" functions as a symbol of the precarious balance of biochemical forces in an exceptional child during puberty. Set apart from his peers by his precocity and by his overactive imagination, Grif finds solitude in nature. Since his mother travels, earth becomes the mother to whom he turns by day and whose presence is keenly realized in his night dreams. Trying to go to sleep is an ordeal because a recurrent note sounds persistently just as the brink is reached. Restless, and driven by a desire to explore the night, on one occasion he stays in the woods in order to experience the thrill of dawn. Standing on the river bank, he hears the sound of "chariot wheels" and the beating hoofs of the great flaming horses as the horsemen are transformed into "a white army retreating in disorder in the field of light" (168–69). As a solitary witness to their rout, he stood on the golden threshold of a summer morning. Plato's myth of the charioteer who controls the image of passion and reason is expanded to its fullest potential as dawn breaks.

Feelings of alienation that alternate with his loneliness lead Grif to seek the company of animals, birds, and even insects; and, sitting beside the river, he becomes "a little river god hugging his knees" (171), watching a dragonfly who is also lonely. Because he feels closer to animals than to humans, his one desire is to learn their language in order to understand the thoughts of those creatures who share his world. Like the primitive Greek animist, he feels a "fellowship with birds and beasts" (171). Since he has no real friend of his own, he creates an imaginary playmate who, like himself, is a "follower of Pan." Because his companion lives somewhere in the woods, he follows the sound of the flute; he knows it will lead him

FORREST REID

"to *the* place, the end of his journey, the home of his hidden friend" (171).

That Grif has a rendezvous with death as he travels to meet what is already stalking him becomes apparent. When Mr. Bradley associates the power of the flute song to return deceased souls to earth and to draw preferred companions beyond earth's boundaries, Grif's anxiety reaches the breaking point. Playing on the child's fear Bradley persists:

He [Billy Tremaine] wants you. You must have put yourself in touch with him some way. He wants you to go away and play with him—where he is now. He finds it hard to come to you, and perhaps he can only do so at certain times. For that matter, the dead are always trying to reach the living. Sometimes they make use of dreams, sometimes they find other ways. He is trying to lure you to him by the sound of his flute, and the more you listen to him the closer he will come to you and the more power he will get over you. (192)

With mounting fear Grif asks what Billy could possibly want of him, to which Bradley replies:

He wants you to be his playmate: he wants to take you into his country. It is not anything dreadful. His country is really here, all around us. Probably he feels lonely. . . . If you are frightened to go with him you must be careful. There is danger everywhere. There is danger in mirrors; there is danger in still waters; there is danger at this moment in sitting talking about him. Do you see how your shadow is lying just across his grave? (192)

When Grif hysterically states that he does not want to die, Bradley declares that "death is nothing . . . all music is a preparation for death . . . a foretaste of it" (193). Then, with the sustained logic of a deranged mind caught in the ecstasy of its own web, Bradley tells Grif that he himself has the power to call up spirits. "Beneath the softness of Bradley's voice lurked something greedy and inhuman, an immense vitality, a kind of feverish flame that lapped against Grif's spirit and withdrew, and advanced again, a resistless, devouring force" (215). Suddenly the graveyard seemed to creep closer until it was just below Grif's window. As Grif becomes more deeply depressed, the magic of the flute disappears, but the mirror in his own room continues to hold a "fatal fascination" for him.

Following his nocturnal adventure, illness strikes Grif. During his uneasy recovery, although Bradley is in his grave, the "Spring

Song" still sounds in Grif's ears from morning to night. "Sometimes he felt that the player on the flute was very near, sometimes he seemed to see him" (302–03). With a terrible insight, he saw at times where he was being drawn; at other times, he could hear in the distance "the low roar of the whirlpool into which he was being sucked; he could feel the overpowering drag of those dark frozen waters" (303). When the burden becomes unbearable, he pours out his story to Miss Nancy, who immediately grasps its horror; "what made it horror was that he himself did not, or could not, perceive it in the light of delusion" (308). Orpheus descends to the depths as death quietly claims Grif and the flute song is heard no more.

Reid uses the flute song, organ music, and the sound of the wind to indicate order and disorder in the minds of Grif and Bradley, in both of whom order is delicately and precariously balanced. The organist maintains a minimum order by playing music in church, but Grif finds primitive order in a benevolent nature that is preferable to the semiordered world of childhood games and to the "Olympian" order of the adult world. Each person has an encounter with reality that destroys his surface order and that culminates in disaster. Grif's beneficent order is destroyed by Bradley's disturbed mind, for he thrusts his obsessions on the mind of a child already overly sensitive to stimuli. Bradley's semiorder is violated when he is forced to face the weird stories he told to Grif and when his mind reverts to the murder of his brother and to the loss of his shadow, which symbolizes damnation. When the church, as the last vestige of his sanctuary, goes, Bradley's outstretched arms symbolize a crucifixion that ironically has been caused by the inability of an overimaginative child to see the organist's stories as delusions. Grif's death, like that of Miles in James's *The Turn of the Screw*, is the price exacted from innocence in its encounter with the violence of experience.

The Spring Song is a frightening adventure in the psychical realm within an otherwise delightful story about happy, carefree children and their very ordinary pastimes. What makes this story so unusual is that Grif's predicament is unknown to either Edward or Barbara, who might have helped him through his difficult transition from boyhood to adolescence. Grif is as inarticulate about his problem of the "ghosts" that haunt his mind as he is about the mystical forces of nature with whom he holds communion. To explain Grif's communication with nature, Reid expertly uses animism as the basis for

his hero's mystical experiences with nature, and for his feeling of
kinship with birds and animals. If it is a sentimental view, as it is,
Reid was not alone in using it. Whereas Norman Douglas in his
Birds and Beasts of the Greek Anthology ignored this view which
disappointed Reid, "the Greeks *had* this feeling of fellowship with
birds and beasts; and certain of their philosophic theories were
founded upon it. . . ."[24] In this novel, Reid conveys his belief imaginatively, sympathetically, and with quiet restraint.

In *Private Road*, Reid noted that although he was interested in
ghosts, haunted houses, and dreams, which he discussed with Walter de la Mare, he was more concerned with a "telepathic communication from a spirit" that seemed to him "both human and divine."
Since he believed that this experience was "part of his real life," and
"had nothing to do with the weaving of tales," he thought it either
"veiled some secret reality" or he himself was "living in a dream."
Feeling that he could never go "beyond the fringe of conjecture" he
was dissatisfied. From time to time he "tried to find in the experience of others an explanation of his own" which, in fact, he never
found (168). While Reid admired the firm convictions of "A.E." and
Basil de Selincourt, both of whom "knew what they believed" and
"could justify" their positions intellectually, he was an agnostic as far
as a creed was concerned. In a letter from de Selincourt in reply to
Reid's questions about the supernatural, de Selincourt wrote that
Reid seemed to lack a "scheme of life" to support his "impressional
representation" of his "personal spiritual experiences"; and that he
appeared to believe in "good and evil spirits who hold intercourse
with men." Parenthetically, Reid replied: "I was never, I think, so
definite as this, and had no experience at all of evil spirits." Whereas
Reid's intuitive belief in immortality was based on his psychic experiences with nature which he characterized as a "feeling of expec-
tancy . . . unaccompanied by fear," de Selincourt's "moral certainty
of immortality" did not satisfy Reid's search.[25]

A closer connection exists between Wordsworth's Pantheism as
an unusual religious experience and Reid's "animistic conception of
nature: something that the listening spirit hears in the sound of the
waves, or feels in the silence of the woods." What Reid most desired
and hoped for was a "revelation" of "beauty and happiness," a
radiance standing far above "a sense of human hauntings with its
concomitant fear, dread, ugliness, gloom, and horror."[26] Reid's art
in *The Spring Song* reveals his ability to heighten the life-affirming

values in Grif's solitary communion with nature, in contrast to the horror of manmade evil that destroys the peace and harmony of the child's world.

The reviews of *The Spring Song* in England indicate its mixed reception by the critical public. One critic wrote that "more than half of Mr. Forrest Reid's story is a pure delight; the rest makes for what we are old-fashioned enough to think unnecessary sadness. . . ."[27] "There are a number of very amusing scenes in the book," another wrote, "and the children's characters, especially Jim and Ann are delightfully drawn. . . . But the author's intentness on the pursuing nightmare robs the later part part of the book of some balance, until Grif's delusions appear real against a rather shadowy background."[28] The periodical and newspaper reviews in America were favorable for the most part. One reviewer wrote that *The Spring Song* is "a heart-breaking little tale. . . . And its poignancy lies in the fineness and restraint of feeling that differentiate it from the coarsely and slushily sentimental child-literature which so often appears to be 'what the people want.' "[29] Another commented that "the story holds the reader's interest firmly from beginning to end. There is about it nothing slovenly or unfinished; the author has the artist's instinct, the artist's loving care, and the result is a book of distinction and charm."[30]

IV Pirates of the Spring

"I don't know why you should take anything more out of it than that Nature did not intend Beach to be a scholar" is the statement with which Reid introduces *Pirates of the Spring* (1919).[31] This work, originally entitled *Beach Traill*, is an autobiographical novel of adolescence that subtly portrays schoolboy friendships and the jealousies, misunderstandings, and fights that are a natural part of them. The central character is Beach Traill, whose personal code of honor and loyalty supports the dominant theme, which is friendship. The slight plot concerns Beach Traill's friendship for Evan Hayes and its difference from his friendship with Miles Oulton or Palmer Dorset, a red-headed boy whom Reid has carried over from *The Spring Song*. The story of changing adolescent friendships is the dominant tale within which Reid portrays a series of incidents: Mr. Oulton's intention to marry the widow Mrs. Traill; Beach's disapproval of this match and his efforts to prevent it; his escapade with Palmer in breaking and entering the Oulton house to retrieve his

photograph, and his confession of guilt; Mrs. Traill's decision to
reject Mr. Oulton's proposal; the classroom episodes with Mr.
Ledgerwood, Mr. Limpet and Dr. Melling; Miles Oulton's fear of his
uncle, on whom he is financially dependent; the formation by the
boys of a Worker's Socialist Club; Palmer Dorset's success in the
expulsion of Cantillon, the "bully"; and Evan Hayes's self-
consciousness about his family's poverty—all are interconnected
episodes in the narrative's pattern. Father O'Brien, a Jesuit priest,
is a friend and adviser to the boys whenever they are in trouble; he
functions as a technical device to advance the plot.

The scene is set in Belfast and Carrick-a-rede, a country district
within walking distance of Osborne, a fashionable school for boys
that is modeled on the Royal Academical Institution, Reid's own
school. From the vantage point of maturity, and as an insider, an
Instonian, Reid recreates his memories of his school days with fondness and admiration. The authenticity of his narrative rings true,
especially in his treatment of Beach's feeling for Evan as it grows
through infatuation and change while affecting his character and his
relation to his peers. To the boys in the school and to Reid himself,
freedom began the moment class was dismissed. For this reason,
and with gentle humor, Reid makes maximum use of the natural,
scenic beauty of Carrick-a-rede as the haven of escape from the
pressures of homework and to contrast the beauty of the countryside
with the grimness of Belfast as a city. The best scenes in the novel
are those in which Reid pictures Beach and Evan together against
the background of this beautiful landscape.

Friendship between Beach and Evan serves not only as a warm,
personal relationship that unites boys from different social
backgrounds, but is also the means for a reconciliation of opposites
in a socioeconomic system that Reid deftly portrays as the story
progresses. With quiet realism, Reid highlights and explores Evan's
confrontation with wealth and poverty in a most unequal world.
Although Evan is a superior day student on scholarship to Osborne,
a wealthy, aristocratic school, his consciousness of the impoverish-
ment of his home environment causes him considerable embarrass-
ment and heartache. By visiting the Traills, he discovers what
wealth means; and his feelings awaken to the soft Spanish beauty of
the lovely Irish lady, Mrs. Traill. A simple factual question from
Mrs. Traill about his schoolwork elicits a dream world opening upon
undiscovered shores. As Evan awakens to love through Mrs. Traill,

Beach awakens to feeling through his friendship with Evan which is revealed in a series of images among which the dream of a boat ride is typical:

They had no need to row, for the boat glided of itself down a dark, smooth, silent river, under great dim boughs in which extraordinary birds of the brightest colours sat swinging above the water. They floated on and on, in the cool, scented shadow, and then suddenly he saw that what he had taken for a particularly brilliant bird was in reality a monstrous scarlet spider, as big as a tea-tray. Before he could reach the rudder they had floated into the web, and the boat came to rest. The shining eyes of the spider fastened on him. The web floated about him, tickling his face and neck, and the more he tried to brush it away the more he got entangled in it. The tickling increased: he jerked his head from side to side to escape it; and opened his eyes (185).

During the summer, the boys explore nature together and enjoy each minute of freedom from school. As summer draws to a close, Reid expresses their relationship with a symbolic description as he depicts the life of the Carrick-a-rede area:

The gulls, drifting out in ever increasing numbers over the blue, wrinkled sea, were whiter still. They were white with the soft whiteness of foam or snow. These birds, and the two boys, were the only living creatures visible in all that wide expanse of sea and land and sky; and the birds were like spirits from some arctic world, who had flown into the summer. They were free and beautiful, detached beings hovering on the fringe of the earth, bright as angels. They wheeled over the water, and suddenly uniting, dropped in a compact flock among the foam in the shallows, filling the air with a harsh exultant crying, ceaseless, eager, voracious (218).

When a storm breaks out, Beach stands in awe of the elements, while Evan is completely frightened. Suddenly Beach sees his relationship to Evan clearly: "He could hear the scream of the witches over the thunder. With his hand on Evan's shoulder, he could feel the nervous tremor that ran through his body, the start with which he recoiled from every flash, and that protective instinct, which had coloured all his friendship, sprang up anew" (226). The friendship between Beach and Evan is different from Beach's relationship to Palmer Dorset or to Miles Oulton; Beach's is intense, emotional, and sentimental—a boyish infatuation.

Beach sees Evan as the ideal of boyhood, the embodiment of

youth: "of an unspoiled beauty, clean and flawless—a beauty that
from its very proportion and harmony gained a kind of spiritual
quality" (89). Against the background of light from a bonfire, Evan
appears strangely different to Beach for "his beauty had, in this
strange light and in these surroundings, a quality that it perhaps
borrowed from them. . . . He looked now like some young faun
who had crept in from the woods, drawn by the bright blaze.
Through the night the murmur of water passed, like a voice from the
beginning of time" (181). Such idealism stands in sharp contrast to
the realistic attitude of Mr. Ledgerwood toward the boys he
teaches: "The human boy was the last animal in the world he was
inclined to view sentimentally. . . . He had little faith in
Wordsworth's 'priest of nature' theory, and still less in the 'trailing
clouds of glory.' The average boy was an indecent little beast, cun-
ning, plausible, callous, with the temperament of a monkey, aggra-
vated by a rudimentary sense of humour, and hardly modified by an
antique and threadbare code of ethics" (83).

At school, Beach is an average student who "trots" Vergil to keep
pace with his class. Through his relationship with Evan, philosophical questions on the mutability of life and beauty, the eternality of
time, and the dimension of "the other" become shared experiences.
Although Beach is an eager disciple, the depths of Evan's understanding evades him. Confronted with the complexity of Platonic
concepts, Beach thinks of Socrates, the ideal teacher, whose dialec-
tical method made deeper problems easier to follow. By the end of
the story, intellectual differences eventually lead to the breaking of
their friendship.

Unlike the friendship of Beach and Evan, that between Beach and
Palmer Dorset is portrayed without sentimentality. To Palmer,
friendship means being a "pal"; it is "something you could rely on
absolutely no matter what you were to do—even if it was murder"
(115). When Palmer supplants Evan as Beach's friend, Reid reveals
his understanding of the shifting and temporary nature of boyhood
friendships as one boy outgrows the other in interest and in experience.

With the pastoral world as background, *Pirates of the Spring* is an
idyll of unusual beauty through which Reid explores changing
friendships as Evan supplants Miles and as Evan is supplanted by
Palmer Dorset. Although nature reflects the harmony of their happiness, it is indifferent to their sufferings; and the inequalities of

social classes mar the scene as they condition and limit Evan's life. Since Evan is part of a deprived minority, he feels class conflicts and religious prejudice more intensely than the Traill family, although they, too, are outsiders, that is Catholics, "among dour Northern Protestants" and "aliens" from Southern Ireland (2). In a ruthless way, Palmer, who can be callous, makes Evan aware of different social classes to which one does or does not belong by placing Evan clearly outside his own class. As change comes to Evan, Beach also feels that change will come in his own house since Mr. Oulton looked at his mother in a "strange" way. To avert the possibility, with malice aforethought, he tips the boat so that Mr. Oulton falls into the water, thus ending the outing before it began. When Oulton refuses to accept defeat, Beach offers to give up all his friends if his mother will only agree to give up one! Ultimately Mrs. Traill rejects Mr. Oulton, but not for Beach's reasons.

Pirates of the Spring shares with *Following Darkness* criticism of a socioeconomic system in which the wealthy live on unearned bounty while the poor literally have no meat for the table. By making the interior of Evan's house so vastly inferior to the beauty of the Traill mansion, which faces the Lagan river, Reid uses houses as symbols of the different social worlds that separate a day boy in a private school from his more wealthy friends. To Evan, Beach's home and garden are a revelation of the social inequality that makes his existence hardly tolerable. In fact, the Traill dinner table, set to impeccable perfection and graced by a beautiful hostess, with grace said in Latin by Father O'Brien, produces in Evan a feeling of unreality that changes to hostility the moment he crosses the threshold of his tenement home: the stain on the tablecloth, "the stupid sickly geranium, the furniture upholstered in black horsehair" become "infinitely distasteful to him" (36–37). He is too embarrassed to ask Beach to dinner, but he ultimately complies with his father's wishes. When Beach visits him, tea and pancakes mark the distance between two worlds. Although Evan hated class distinctions, he was a helpless victim of circumstances unlikely to change.

Despite Russell Burlingham's statement that *Pirates of the Spring* reveals an "exhausted imagination,"[32] this novel shows Reid's ability to portray subleties of friendship between schoolboys. If it is a variation on the same theme, he nevertheless conveys the mood of a Theocritean idyll disturbed only by social inequalities that ring true;

he presents a study of some depth of character development during the diverse stages of adolescent turmoil; and he handles the changing friendships that occur among schoolboys delicately, sensitively, and with occasional touches of humor and irony. Moreover, his ability to enter empathetically into the mind and feelings of Beach, Miles, Palmer, and Evan, to portray the subtle change each boy undergoes in response to friendship, leaves the reader with the conviction that truth is achieved through the narrator's firm control of his subject.

Both in England and in America *Pirates of the Spring* was favorably reviewed on the whole. A British reviewer wrote that *"Pirates of the Spring* is a thoughtful story about schoolboys written for adults," but he was critical of Reid's character portrayal except for the priest who is "treated with sympathy."[33] In America, Reid received appreciative reviews of this novel. Two reviewers described it as a "narrative of quiet beauty."[34] By another it was characterized as having a "higher degree of artistry" than Richard Pryce's *Christopher*, Hugh Walpole's *Jeremy*, or E. F. Benson's *David Blaize*.[35] A fourth critic commented on "the added pleasure" given "in its description of the countryside," and called it "an artistic delight."[36]

V   Pender Among the Residents

Pender Among the Residents (1922)[37] is Reid's first direct study of the occult and the psychic as the supernatural dimension of his Realistic novel. The title functions on three levels: Pender Kilmartin's relationship to kith and kin, to his friends and neighbors, and to ancestral ghosts who return to the manor house Ramoan to reenact the tragedy and romance of their past lives. On the psychological level, the novel is the story of Pender's haunted mind. Set in Ballycastle, a seaside resort, shortly after World War I, the narrative begins with Pender's homecoming in early autumn, flashes back to his childhood, goes forward to Easter before the war, and ends in spring of the next year. Interior time is portrayed when Pender writes his memoirs in which past becomes present as the drama unfolds.

The permanent residents at Ballycastle include Pender, the young bachelor squire just returned from the war; Miss Foy, a gentle impoverished music teacher and the former secretary to Pender's grandfather, Edward Kilmartin; Dr. Olphert, Pender's childhood friend and physician; the Reverend Mr. Burton, a canon who is manipulated by his domineering, shrewd, match-making wife Nellie, who is a cousin to Pender and who, having managed her daughter Norah's engagement to Pender, is now bent on engineering their marriage. Other characters include Mrs. O'Clery, aunt to George Best who is in love with Norah; Captain Chaffinch who prefers golf to literary society meetings where Mrs. Burton reads boring papers; Professor Heron and his prodigy son Trefusis; Tonie Ronayne and her bulldog Tim whose fights with Mrs. Burton's dog Wopsey provide the comedy. Finally, the ancestral ghosts of Roxana, of her jealous husband Edward Kilmartin, and of his half brother Tom Febris, who was Roxana's young lover, play a significant role. Mrs. West, the old family housekeeper, and Miss Foy, the former family secretary, serve the author as a link with the past because of their relationship with the Kilmartin household.

The major plot develops Nellie Burton's efforts to arrange a marriage between Pender and Norah who is really in love with George Best. The subplot reveals the process by which Pender realizes Norah's infidelity; refuses to accept a marriage of convenience; and, through his generosity, makes the marriage of George and Norah possible. Within this love plot, the ancestral ghosts of Pender's relatives, the Kilmartins, reenact the romance and the tragedy of their lives; and their action begins when Pender falls in love with Roxana, his great-aunt by marriage, whose story he attempts to write. Old memoirs and letters discovered in the attic, the illicit love affair of Roxana Kilmartin with her husband's half brother Tom Febris, the discovery of their liaison by a spy planted in the house by her husband Edward Kilmartin, the murder of the witness, and the burial of his body by both husband and lover in the ground of the estate, provide the psychic dimension of the story. The romance and the tragedy of the Ramoan house as an ancestral curse on marriage go back to the Edward Kilmartin affair; and they plague Pender's mother who, by marrying outside her class, is disinherited; and they threaten to descend on Pender. By writing Roxana's story, Pender is possessed by her so much that his mind is literally "away" from his body. Roxana's situation then becomes the past equivalent of the present clandestine relationship between Norah and George—one which Pender grasps through psychic communication.

The novel is divided into eleven parts that present external and internal action in a series of scenes in which distance is economically controlled by four houses within which the action occurs. The Ramoan, Heron, Burton, and Foy houses reflect the character of the residents who occupy them as well as their social status. The Ramoan estate represents the landed aristocracy; the Heron, upper middle class; the Burton, middle class; and the Foy house, one rented and about to be sold.

At the opening of the story the reader sees Pender and Norah through Dr. Olphert's eyes. Pender is a sensual ascetic whom his friend cannot imagine as Norah's lover. Norah appears to be "unapproachable," like Prosper Merimée's "La Vénus d'Ille" (25), in which a woman suffocated her young bridegroom in her bronze arms because he had placed "a wedding ring on her finger."[38] As Reid's story develops, Pender's subconscious fear of marriage is portrayed in a series of images beginning with his earliest memories of his mother's unfortunate marriage and her subsequent disinheritance. By the use of Henry Vaughan's "The Retreat," Pender's longing to escape to happy days of childhood represents the beginning of his withdrawal from a forthcoming marriage without love. A quotation from Poe's "The Sleeper" reveals his fear that Norah may discover a past that he prefers to keep to himself:

> I pray to God that she may lie
> Forever with unopened eye
> While the dim sheeted ghosts go by.[39]

Having lingered too long in San Miniato on the Arno, Pender's too hastily made engagement to Norah becomes difficult to break. His fourteen months of separation from his fiancee "counted like fourteen years" (62), for he preferred the company of beautiful women with "pale hands," a delicate purity "as follows on a spent wave of passion" (59–60). Since Norah's ambitions war with Pender's literary interests, incompatibility of temperament is an obvious barrier to marriage. Like the romantic Prufrock, whom he closely resembles, he prefers friendship to a marriage that makes demands to which he feels unequal.

Several images foreshadow the separation of Pender and Norah, but they also advance the theme of withdrawal. First Pender sees Norah as "a remote passionless Diana on a moonlit hill" (69); when they walk along the cliffs of Kebane, the black rocks of Fair Head chimeralike seem to be some universal force of destruction, and Norah becomes "Diana the huntress" (141–42). When he kisses her on the cheek, he has placed their relationship where he wants it to be; for, since he has "played on the fiddle" to Roxana, he can hardly come back (194). In a melodramatic scene in the rain, Norah tells George that she intends to marry Pender because she cannot be a poor man's wife; but Pender knows of her infidelity and refuses her letter of compromise. At the novel's end, Pender is recovering from a nightmare in which the ghosts of his ancestors reenact the sordid drama of their violent affair. Pender, who has now passed through the veil, knows that they can no longer control his life; and he and Miss Foy leave shortly thereafter for Italy.

As for the pattern of ancestral hauntings, there is always a witness. Mrs. West knew of the background of the Kilmartin house, as did Miss Foy, but neither was aware of its sinister depths. The observer who witnessed the liaison between Tom and Roxana paid with his life, and Roxana died shortly afterward. Trefusis, the child poet, sees Norah and George at the cottage, confronts Norah with what he has seen, and tells Miss Richardson, the village gossip. Pender has "seen" and written his story of the fatal woman Roxana which will continue to live in *Pender Among the Residents.*

In order to control and expand the infidelity theme, Reid uses the overarching myth of Lamia, the serpent woman, which is supported by the fatal woman motif of Mérimée, Poe, Coleridge, and Keats. Since the original source of the Lamia story is taken from Philostratus, the persistence of infidelity from past to present time becomes the archetypal pattern for the character of Norah as Lamia, Pender as Lycius, and Dr. Oliphert as the wise philosopher. In the Classical myth, Lamia is transformed by Hermes from a serpent into a beautiful woman who seduces a young Corinthian, Lycius, and who is finally unmasked at the wedding banquet by the sage Apollonius. When he pierces through her disguise, she vanishes as quickly as she had come. Reid states the Lamia myth in the context of the novel when Pender and Dr. Oliphert discuss the relationship between Roxana and Tom. Oliphert notes that, when Apollonius unveils the serpent, he found that "all her furniture was like Tantalus' gold . . . no substance but mere illusion" (199). To Pender, "He [Lycius] was saved from the serpent and there are things worse than death" (199). From the moment that Pender begins to write Roxana's story, his consciousness of the affair between Norah and George starts to surface. When Dr. Oliphert says, "I distrust her" (199), Roxana and Norah are linked together. A verse from Poe's

"Ulalume" that warns the lover of a star whose "pallor I strangely mistrust" advances the theme of the faithless woman that organizes the novel.[40]

Through the medium of a novel being written within a novel and with a poem in process by Trefusis, the child prodigy from Belfast, Reid is able to comment on the artistic imagination at work. By using a mirror image, he portrays his   efforts to write a novel of occult and psychic phenomena when Pender creates his romance. Between the conception of the Roxana tale and its realization, Pender attempts to instruct Trefusis as to the proper way to write poetry. Using a myth and several hints for procedure, Pender has the boy work on a poem from Plutarch, which brings the reader back to the Greek world at the same time that it reveals Reid's attitude toward poetry and imaginative prose. "If you do write it, remember this time you are writing for me," Pender counsels. "What difference does that make?" asked Trefusis. "It must be done in my way," Pender insists, "otherwise I shan't pay for it. You must try to see it and hear it and feel it and smell it before you even begin. And there must be no poetic language—not a word" (170). When Trefusis asks what Pender means by poetry, he replies: "A mysterious thing . . . a mixture of enchantment and music— something immensely primitive—a survival—old—old as Egyptian magic," or, we may add, Greek myth (173).

Pender Among the Residents had a mixed reception from reviewers and readers. The occult theme used to comment on the relationship of Pender and Norah demands considerable concentration and a willingness to grant psychic communication as a means of understanding. Of Reid's ability to treat the occult, an anonymous reviewer in the *New York Times* wrote that "There is no one writing today who exceeds him [Reid] in the ability to deal effectively, persuasively, with occult themes."[41] Another critic felt that Reid would have written a better novel had he kept the romantic mystery and the supernatural fantasy for another book.[42] "Professional" and "invented" were Reid's own terms of dissatisfaction with his efforts. Since he did not believe in its "rather conventional ghost story," he knew it was unsuccessful.[43] Despite its faults, the Lamia myth is functional; the characters are round rather than flat; and the socioeconomic levels of life are portrayed convincingly by Miss Foy, whose meagre pension scarcely enables her to buy margarine; by the Burtons, who are social climbers; and by Pender, who inherits

Ramoan, though it too is deteriorating. The background of nature, the light and shadow, the contrasting and opposing forces that are part of Reid's art are all here. The picture of the child prodigy Trefusis, modeled on Romney Robinson of Belfast, and his father, Professor Heron (W. W. Skeat), are in the best tradition of character portrayal.[44] However, this story is not so successful as Reid's previous works because he does not have the ability to depict adult life and relationships with the same imaginative intensity with which he treats boyhood and adolescence.

CHAPTER 5

The Milk of Paradise:
The Major Novels (1927–1947)

WHEN Reid's intellectual commitment to the myths of Greece
had become total, his major novels from *Demophon* (1927) to
Young Tom (1944), including *Uncle Stephen* (1931), *Brian Westby*
(1934), and *The Retreat* (1936), reveal a firm control of technique
and a clarity of perspective that represents the fulfillment of a
lifetime dedicated to imaginative fiction. *Demophon* is the first fruit
of the harvest where Greek myth shows the esemplastic power of
Reid's mythopoeic imagination that probes the deepest truths that
feeling grasps before intellect knows. Once again, youth is his subject, through whose eyes the measure of the world is derived.
Dream is the shape that Reid's meaning takes as hope for a better
world. Since Reid was a time-haunted man, we find that experiments with time and with time travel are essential aspects of his
technique.

Brian Westby, a novel about friendship and the creative process,
gives the reader directions should he wish to see the Greek ideal as
it evolves from beginning to end. Even if the reader were to read
only the *Tom Barber* trilogy, Reid's vision comes through un-
equivocally. To read *Young Tom*, *The Retreat*, and *Uncle Stephen* is
the more logical order if we wish to follow Tom from boyhood to
adolescence; but Reid wrote them in reverse sequence, and each is
complete in itself. His ability to capture the essence of childhood
and the "felt thought" of exceptional young adults is unequaled in
originality and in sensitivity. Happiness radiates throughout his
pages where dream and reality interpenetrate and where the supernatural and the natural world meet. To find a modern novelist with
deeper Humanistic values would be difficult, and Reid's major
novels may at last have the success denied them during his lifetime
when the spiritual quality of his persistent vision has been recognized.

I   Demophon

Demophon: A Traveller's Tale (1927)[1] is a fictionalized version of *Apostate* in which Reid is the young boy Demophon; Hermes, his dream playmate; and Emma, Demeter. Based on the Demeter myth in *The Greek Anthology*, Ovid's *Metamorphoses*, and Walter Pater's "The Myth of Demeter and Persephone,"[2] *Demophon* is a romantic odyssey that embodies Reid's total commitment to Greece as the functioning symbol of his landscape and values. As portrayed through the mind and experiences of Demophon, his journey from Eleusis to the mountains of Thessaly and back becomes the education of a child in Humanistic values; for he learns them directly from his encounter with great and wise teacher-philosophers.

The epigraph on the title page of *Demophon* records the myth from which Reid began: "But of Demophon, the son of Keleos, it is said that when he grew to boyhood he wandered from his father's house, and because of something divine in him, met with divine adventures." Reid added to this myth the figure of Hermes, a divine playmate, counterpart of "the spirit I prayed to in my boyhood."[3] In Greek mythology, Hermes is "a God of dreams, . . . a boy God . . . a protector of boys."[4] Although Reid maintained that he knew little about Hermes except for the Classical myth, he certainly knew the Symbolist movement from his background reading, from the sources he uses, and from his correspondence with Arthur Symons. Symbolist literature in Europe and America during the late nineteenth and twentieth centuries reveals considerable preoccupation with Occultism, which is "the metaphysical foundation of the Symbolist movement" in which Hermes is a significant figure.[5]

Since Reid uses a mythical mode to explore ideas in *Demophon*, the consequences of his perception place him in the tradition of visionaries from William Blake to the present who "hoped to change this world" by transforming "the quality of men's consciousness."[6] Although Reid cites a parallel to Hermes in the story of Tobias and the angel from what he calls Christian mythology, the Tobias source is not Christian but Old Testament Apocrypha. His use of the Hermes myth, like Rainer Maria Rilke's use of "angel," functions as a symbol of a supernatural dimension in the natural. It is also similar to Emmanuel Swedenborg's communication with angels and spirits in the "realms of light,"[7] but Reid's Hermes symbolizes a search for a spirit in nature, for a divine friend, and for the integration of per-

sonality. As a Doppelgänger, he is the spiritual aspect of the physical self.[8] The ecumenical symbolism of Hermes as a bridge to religious unity has been carefully documented in the scholarly work of
A. J. Festugière, who explores the occult meaning in a manner
comparable to Reid's use of this myth.[9] The closest sculptural source
that Reid mentions is the Hermes of Praxiteles.[10]

From the opening line of *Demophon*, the reader is transported to
Greece; and, for the duration of one year, he never once leaves the
"golden isles": "Beyond the grove of laurels sacred to Artemis lay a
blue, crinkled sea. It glittered dazzlingly in the hot sunshine; and far
out in the bay where water and sky met, the dark rocks of Salamis
rose like a dream-land, because a God had dropped a haze about
them" (13). Details drawn from the everyday life of an agricultural
people give an earthiness to this imaginative tale. Keleos, Demophon's father, on the threshold of old age, seems like a figure of
Father Time as he walks home with his daughter, who "rubbed a
dirty hand" across a "very dirty face" (14). His "beard was grizzled,
his skin tanned like leather, and the sweat ran in beads from the
roots of his matted hair" (14). Reid captures with this figure of
venerable old age with a child by the hand the simplicity of a rustic
character who takes his nobility from the earth itself. Again, in an
image of fields "yellow with ripened corn" until "the spirit of the
great earth mother passed over them changing their color," Reid
paints a description of earth's fertility and bounty (14).

Within Demophon's educational odyssey, Reid thematically
structures a search for spiritual meaning as a search for a divine
friend. Like each of Reid's imaginative, exceptional boy heroes,
Demophon is marked by "a touch of the divine" that makes him
different from ordinary boys. Demeter, the goddess earth mother,
saved him from death by anointing his body in fire which purged
grossness and sensuality from it. Because his mother Metanira in-
terrupted the deification process, Demophon feels incomplete and
lonely; and, when his cosmic and personal loneliness cries for companionship, his desire brings Hermes from the woods. Hermes, a
boy of Demophon's age, is first called brother and later friend; he
appears whenever Demophon needs him; and by the end of the
story Hermes promises to remain forever with him. To Demophon,
Hermes is "the most wonderful person in the world. He could make
toys out of wood or clay or pomegranate skin; he made a pipe of
hemlock stalks (binding the hollow stems with white wax), and when

it was finished he showed Demophon how to blow out of it musical sounds. He taught him how to throw a spinning quoit; he taught him how to run and leap and wrestle and box and swim; he turned the sylvan glade into a green gymnasium and Demophon himself into the smallest of small athletes" (31).

When Hermes leaves, as he occasionally must, Demophon becomes discontented with farm chores, with school, and particularly with his teacher Pittacus. Demophon's dreams of a terrestrial paradise replace humdrum reality as the climate of Pindar's "Sixth Pythian Ode" guarantees perpetual fertility for the fruits of the earth and complete freedom for its inhabitants. Under fair skies there are "fields of crimson roses, and three times a year the trees bear fruit. No storms blow there, and there is no snow. But neither is it too hot. The land is never parched, and the sea-wind breathes softly through the branches. There by the streams that flow through the green meadows, everyone is happy after his own fashion—making music or poetry, or wrestling or playing games, or running races, or dancing—and the lover is with his beloved" (55). In this passage, three threads of the story meet in an apostrophe to freedom: Demophon's search for his divine friend Hermes; the theme of an earthly paradise as the land of heart's desire; and the concept of divinity in humanity. Shortly thereafter, during a ceremony symbolizing primitive initiation rites of passage from childhood to puberty, Demophon dedicates his hair to the sea. He then sets out on his romantic adventures in search of his lost playmate, Hermes.

Although this odyssey takes only one year, it covers extensive geography. On his journey, he encounters mythical creatures whose divided natures reveal their loneliness. When Pholos, the centaur, who is a "shy beautiful creature," approaches Demophon reluctantly because of his fear of being hurt, he tells Demophon that: "Boys and even men . . . are inclined to snatch up stones when they see anyone who is not the same as themselves" (49–50). This lesson in tolerance of anomaly is repeated when Demophon next encounters Glaukos, half man and half fish, who is condemned to spend his days beneath the sea pining away for his beloved Scylla. When Demophon tells Glaukos of his search for Hermes, Glaukos tells him that "it is better not to look for people. For when you find them, they don't want you. Scylla is lost because I loved her" (113). Leaving Glaukos, Demophon passes over the mountains sacred to Pan where he sees a bacchanalian orgy in which passionate females in a wild rhythmic dance evoke "their dark ambiguous God and the fructifying powers of Earth" (70). Dancing until they drop on the grass from exhaustion, they lay "with swimming eyes and panting limbs" (72–73). As a feeling of aversion sweeps over him, Demophon turns his eyes from the "shameful and degrading" sight with a disgust that "follows gratified curiosity" (73). His only wish is to see Hermes face to face.

Before Demophon can be united with Hermes, however, he has to travel farther to gain knowledge of nature as his preparation for the wisdom he learns from two Greek philosophers, Euphorion of Ephesos, the illustrious Sophist, and Sophron, the philosopher-sage. Although Demophon is captured by pirates and retained in the house of Laomedon, the priest of death, he escapes unscathed. Walking along the river, he has a mystical experience in which he feels the unity of life in the spirit of nature; he suddenly knows that "he and the snakes and the lizards and the colored butterflies and even the earth over which he walked were one" (192). When the animistic feeling of unity with earth is accepted by Demophon, the turning point in his search for religious values is reached. Although he has found his roots in nature, he has to face and understand the question of self-identity:

What was it—this something that was not his mind, that was even closer to him than his mind? It dwelt in him: it was the sadness which rose and mingled with the beauty that flowed in through his eyes from the summer fields, and through his ears from the wind and the sea: it was his longing for his lost playmate, his love for those spotted snakes, his friendship with this tiny flying beetle that had settled on his hand. It dwelt in him; but might it not be truer to say that it *was* Demophon? His home really was, then, in those far-off islands in the West; and he was not setting out on a journey, but going back, going home. (183–84)

Demophon's mystical experience of nature prepares his background for the philosophical teaching of Sophron—the means with which Reid comments on war, violence, and religious sacrifice. From Sophron, Demophon learns to differentiate between appearance and reality, to understand the evolutionary life force in which "a plant becomes an animal, . . . an animal becomes a plant" (195). He also learns that there is no perfection or happiness on earth, no fulfillment of natural desire, because religions have promoted and condoned blood sacrifice and wars without end. Sophron's concept of a golden age where blood sacrifice no longer exists is Reid's vision of a Utopia that is described by Sophron to Demophon as "a single community which embraced heaven and earth," in which "gods and men and animals were united in friendship and order and temperance" (197). Finally Demophon comes to realize that happiness has to be sought within the self.

Demophon's next adventure is to attend a ceremonial honoring Adonis that is expressive of the god's dual nature that Demophon rejects as a cult of physical desire and death. What he sees confirms the teaching of Euphorion, who had spoken derisively of any cult from the East that is a religion of death; for Euphorion believes that religion should be "a preparation for life" (207). The doctrine of metempsychosis underlying Euphorion's belief in his own past identity as "a fish, a tortoise, a lynx, an eagle, a girl, a boy" is much more acceptable to Demophon than any blood sacrifice (215). By far the most important lesson that Demophon learns is that conscience, the inner light, involves lifelong education, and that he who would grow from a lower to a higher self must follow conscience which dictates kindness to persons and animals as being more basic than any divine compensation awaiting man could be.

In a final encounter, Demophon meets Xanthus, the sex-goddess enchantress, who takes him prisoner for purposes of seduction; but his reaction to her wiles and tricks results only in repulsion and aversion—"this real love-making bored him" (242). After his escape from Xanthus, Demophon feels as if a guardian spirit—"an angel, a God, a protector, a lover"—has been with him throughout all his dangers. As he kneels by the wayside shrine and prays to Hermes, the boy god comes to him; and "though he was older and somewhat graver . . . he was a youth, a young shepherd, he was still the boy who had come to him in the woods, his lost playmate, his hero, his friend" (266).

Although Hermes cannot remain with him for long, he plucks a golden hair from his head and places it among Demophon's black ones. "And now you are indisputably mine . . . marked with my mark," he said, and "not all the kings of the earth could remove it. I will tell you further, that I myself, even if I desire to, could not remove it, for our laws are not like your laws, and what we have once decreed is unalterable":

It is there for ever. I have done, though in a different way, something of what Deo tried to do. Just exactly what she had planned can never now be done: that promise that at the appointed time I shall come again for you; and that in the end all will be well. . . . And now we had better be starting on our journey. I am going to see you safely home, and though at your father's gate I must say good-bye, the whole long day is before us.

So they set out together, hand in hand, through the waving barley fields. (269)

By following Demophon's "divine" adventures in his search for his lost playmate Hermes, it becomes evident that Reid is concerned with a search for the nature of reality and with a discovery of personal identity. When Demophon discovers his own identity and realizes that there are creatures in the animal world with whom he has something in common (Glaukos and Pholos), one aspect of his journey is fulfilled. When he accepts this fact, he knows that he may achieve happiness if he looks for it "where it really is . . . within himself" (196).

In addition to the friendship theme, Reid portrays the value of natural religion that affirms joy, spontaneity, and life rather than a faith that looks forward to death. That all levels of being find unity in earth whose spirit is a life-giving force is Reid's belief and Demophon's discovery. From this point of view, Hermes functions as an occult symbol for a principle of unity that is basic to religious experience. Demophon's search for Hermes is the search for a reality of spirit in nature itself. Just as dreams were one means by which primitive man came to believe in the existence of spirit, Demophon's dreams give assurances of the reality of a presence outside himself that corresponds to the spirit within.

Through the Demeter myth, Reid found a symbol to organize and explore the fundamental unity of spirit underlying matter and appearance, infusing all levels of life, and uniting the outward and inward worlds in its harmony. The end of man's adventures becomes, therefore, a realization of self in relation to the spirit that gives unity to life. On a personal level, conscience takes priority over law, custom, and institutional religions as it must if the world is to survive.

Demophon indicates Reid's advance with technique because he tells the story from Demophon's point of view, at his own level, and with no intrusion on the author's part. The style is clear, simple, and direct; the prose has a natural rhythm that fits the characters; and nature is painted in rich, varied, and sensuous colors. Reid's feeling for Greek life and thought is so organic that we sense his security in his discovery of a race, a creed, and a way of life to which he believed he belonged. Because of the primitive Greek animistic approach to nature, he shared a " 'sense of fellowship with every scaled and furred and feathered creature.' "[11] If his passionate love of youth, which almost approaches a cult of Hermes, is in harmony with the Greek attitude toward all young, supple forms, it is also shared by very ordinary persons to whom children and animals are the heritage of the Lord.'

II   Uncle Stephen

Uncle Stephen (1931),[12] the first novel of the *Tom Barber* trilogy, was originally entitled *My Uncle's a Magician* to emphasize Tom's pride in his only blood relative. When first written, the novel was, as Reid described it, "a dream story . . . from beginning to end . . . composed in sleep . . . or 'lived' for I undoubtedly was Tom."[13] Unfortunately, Reid destroyed the first draft, which necessitated reworking the final story to the point where he was unable to separate the "true dream from the novel" that is the dream experience. In a story of "magic and mystery," Uncle Stephen's generosity to Tom is the dream center. In the original dream version Reid used physical metamorphosis to portray Uncle Stephen as the boy he was at nineteen; in the present novel, the boy "Philip," who is Uncle Stephen Collet as a boy, replaces the original dream relationship. Since both stories treat "sacred and profane love," the machinery is merely a way of telling the same story. Viewed in this light, Reid maintained that the inner truth of the narrative was as little affected by external improbabilities as were Socrates's tales of Egypt. The emotion that the novel symbolizes is as real as Tom, through whose imagination the story is told, even if he is "a rather special little boy, who 'felt through all this earthly dress bright shoots of everlastingness.' "[14]

Because Reid feared ridicule, he suppressed the original dedication to Hermes, his "tutelary spirit"; he substituted quotations from the Book of Job and from Wordsworth's "Michael" to reenforce the theme of desire and fulfillment as the metaphysical framework which the novel explores:

O that I might have my request; and that
God would grant me the thing I long for!
. . . .
They were as companions. . . .
Objects which the shepherd loved before
Were dearer now. . . . From the boy there came
Feelings and emanations—things that were
Light to the sun and music to the wind;
And the old man's heart seemed born again.[15]

On the day of Tom's father's funeral, the thought of living at
Gloucester Terrace with his stepmother, with her family, and with
his stepuncle Horace Gurney impels Tom to run away to his mater-
nal Uncle Stephen. As his stepfamily discusses what to do with Tom,
his own plans for a journey take shape. Aided by his stepsister Jane,
who loves Tom, he takes the railway coach to Kilbarron, where at
the station he meets the Reverend Charles Quentin Knox, his uncle's friend. Finally, when he arrives late at night at Uncle Stephen's
estate, Tom is greeted by Mrs. Deverell, the housekeeper, and is
informed that Uncle Stephen is expecting him.

Known to the villagers as an eccentric recluse and as a magician,
Uncle Stephen lives on a large estate with a carriage house attached
to it. The house is a survival from Gothic Romance with its secret
passages and its inner sanctuary where Uncle Stephen keeps a fragmented statue of Hermes. In the original dream version, the room
was a temple containing a "black marble beast, the crouching beast
of *Apostate*."[16] Uncle Stephen's warm welcome and concern for
Tom is so much like magic that rapport between the two is instan-
taneous. Since Uncle Stephen is a Greek scholar, he shares his
knowledge of Greek myth, literature, and religion with his eager
nephew. While Uncle Stephen takes a short business trip, Tom
explores the estate, the woods, and the river; and he discovers in
the garden the statue of a boy holding an urn. In the carriage house,
he meets another runaway boy, "Philip Coombe"; and this new
friend becomes Tom's soulmate. By metamorphosis in dream time,
the boy Stephen,"Philip Coombe," is Uncle Stephen recapturing
his boyhood. Tom sleeps with "Philip" in Uncle Stephen's sanctuary
and journeys with him to Coombe Bridge to verify their ancestry;
but, at this point in the dream Philip ships out to sea and Uncle
Stephen returns home. Meanwhile, Tom also strikes a friendship

with Jim Deverell, a "poacher" who is rescued from the hands of the law by money that Tom borrows from Uncle Stephen.

Prior to Uncle Stephen's return, Tom prays to Hermes and discovers the archetypal patterns of identity between Hermes the protector of youth, Uncle Stephen, the adolescent Stephen, the urn god, Tom himself, and perhaps Deverell too. When Uncle Stephen appears, Tom knows that his uncle is "his master" and that he is his willing "pupil" (268). By the end of the novel, Uncle Stephen is making plans to adopt Tom and to travel with him to Southern Europe and the Italian coast, where the realities of the Greek way of life await them, far from the provincial world of Kilbarron and from Uncle Horace at Gloucester Terrace.

In *Uncle Stephen*, Reid thematically explores a boy's search for a father figure and a childless man's search for a son. The companionship that each finds in the other, despite the disparity of age, is lyrically portrayed. Within the novel, Hermes is the symbol that organizes past and present time to project the future. Dream psychology, both primitive and modern, is used to advance the internal action. As a result of this use of Hermes and dream, the novel may be read both as an experiment in time and as a parapsychological study of dream states.

From beginning to end of the novel, the inner world of dream is a retreat from death, fear, and loneliness. The opening scene portrays Tom's emotional turmoil at his father's grave as the clergyman intones the prayers for the dead, sending forth his father's soul on his "perilous and distant journey" (34). "*This* was not like 'Ulalume'— this ugly varnished brass-handled box covered with flowers" . . . that "somehow increased its ghastliness." The men "hired to bear the burden depressed and exasperated him. If anybody really cared! . . . Death was the triumph of clay and worms, and the horrors that were already at work out of sight. . . . It's ugliness had been revealed suddenly . . . as if he had come on an obscene inscription or picture chalked upon a wall" (339–40).

From a religious ceremony that stressed resurrection in a future life Tom turned away; he fixed "his attention on a creamy blackspotted butterfly who . . . like a little soul newly exiled from the body . . . alit on a stock of foxgloves and became . . . a comfortable earthly creature warm with appetites, eager, impatient, purposeful, as he explored cave after purple cave, forcing an entrance, greedy, determined" (340). By rejecting orthodox religious dogma about death, Tom also rejects a religion that denies the positive life force by its emphasis on life hereafter. If the butterfly symbolizes the natural soul, then animism is his adopted religion. Since Tom had no love for his father in life, he is unmoved by his death. The unexpressed conflict between father and son is revealed through a stream of consciousness as Tom remembers a continual atmosphere of "spiritual remoteness" in which his father was always "extraordinarily unapproachable" (341). When Mr. Barber had remarried, Tom had felt not only alienated by his stepfamily but different from his stepbrothers Eric and Leonard. In refusing to accept the world of the Gavney-Barbers, he contacts by telepathic communication his only genuine relation, Stephen Collet, to whom he knows he belongs.

The sexual imagery of the butterfly passage is repeated in two additional life-enhancing male dominating images: first, the image of grasshoppers as "tiny men dressed in green, sharpening their knives and scissors for other insects"; second, the image of "a blue dragon-fly, like a shining airman," flies from its "breeding place among the reeds on the lake. He had an impression of emerging from some choking stagnant valley of death into the world of life" (343). These two images contrast sharply with the way Tom sees his stepmother, whose movements resembled a cow "heavy and indolent, yet not ungraceful," who suggested "milk" (346). At Kilbarron, Tom finds a home in a world of natural beauty which Reid identifies as the "Greek" landscape—the country of his dreams where normal life processes are no threat.

The second half of the novel organizes what Reid calls the ideal he tried to express "naked and complete,"[17] the relationship between Uncle Stephen and Tom, master and pupil, through his use of a Greek world view. By means of the characters of Tom and Uncle Stephen, Reid once again explores the conflict between Christianity and Humanism. Tom, like Uncle Stephen, rejects Christian dogma for animism in religion and for Humanism as a life philosophy. When Tom leaves Gloucester Terrace by running away to Kilbarron, thereby repeating the pattern of Uncle Stephen's youth, the values Tom finds with his uncle are rooted in Greek antiquity; for friendship is the highest human relationship and faithfulness the most important virtue. The natural country setting of Kilbarron, with its honeysuckle and beech trees, becomes the natural countryside of Greece; the shrill hidden orchestra of grasshoppers played their ancient Greek melody broken only by the notes of a cuckoo whose monstrous song resembles "clock-time." On the banks of the river, with the sun on his body, Tom tried to imagine the sun as God and hoped that "a God might come to him out of the river" (395).

Tom's education in Greek world values comes through Stephen Collet's book on Greek mythology and religion although its title is not stated. From the master's conversations, he learns that behind mythological tales and stories lies a spiritual world that is closer to the earth than the remote heaven of Christianity where powers and influences are paramount. When Tom also discovers the three commandments of Triptolemos, he prefers them to the Ten Commandments of Moses: "Honour your father and mother. Offer fruit to the gods. Be kind and just to animals." These are sensible ethical imperatives that reduce the burden considerably, since three principles could be "absolutely kept." As for laws, they are a question of temperament to Tom (418).

Central to the inner story, a fragmented statue of Hermes in Uncle Stephen's room sets the religious atmosphere for Tom's gradual acceptance of Humanism. In its presence, Tom feels as if he is born again to a new kingdom of infinite possibilities, although it demands secrecy of its initiates. In Uncle Stephen's absence, although Tom's relationship with Deverell deepens, the experiment of sleeping in the presence of Hermes with young Stephen fails to occur. Medieval magic, Uncle Stephen tells Tom later, is a black kind when it is compared to the magic of Greek antiquity. When Tom asks about magic, Uncle Stephen replies:

I dare say Homer believed in the magic of Kirke, but I don't think Euripides believed in the magic of Medea. Doubtless there were real women, who, like the woman in the poem of Theocritus, turned a magic wheel to charm back a lost lover. But all that is utterly different from medieval magic, with its conscious evil and depraved association with Christianity. Apollonius of Tyana was called a magician, but he and his master Pythagoras were really holy men, and if supernatural powers were attributed to them it was because they were in communication with the Gods, not with evil spirits. (443)

In this discussion, Apollonius of Tyana and Pythagoras emerge as holy men with whom Uncle Stephen belongs because of his commitment to the religious values that Hermes symbolizes. It also

becomes obvious that Uncle Stephen will pass on the torch of learning, experience, and authenticity to Tom who will transmit in time
the heritage to other disciples.

By use of time past as dream time, reenacted in an existential
present and extending to a future planned by Uncle Stephen, Reid
controls his story. Some credibility is lost, however, when Uncle
Stephen cannot remember the events preceding the night on which
Tom returned from Coombe Bridge. Within the dream time sequence, each relationship of Tom to Deverell, to Stephen (Philip),
and to Uncle Stephen is a repetition of the primal act involving
collaboration and consent in a pattern of eternal recurrence. Tom's
love for Deverell, who is hunted by the police; the money that
Uncle Stephen gives knowingly to insure Deverell's escape; Tom's
love for Stephen (Philip), who leaves to go to sea; and Tom's love for
Uncle Stephen are variations on the same theme of homoeroticism.
The use of the journey to Coombe Bridge taken by Tom and
Stephen (Philip) is simply the means of verifying Uncle Stephen's
idenity as the wayward son of Henry Collet.

In the final scene, in which plans for a trip to Southern Italy and
the Italian coast become definite and in which the adoption papers
are finalized, Tom stands in imagination beside Uncle Stephen "gaz-
ing at the ruins of the Parthenon, sitting beside him on the shore of
the Sicilian sea, far, far away from all this, under a bluer sky and a
hotter sun . . ." (567). The landscape is drawn from remembered
"fragments of Theocritus" and from recollections of "a walk taken by
Socrates and Phaidros along the banks of Ilissos, and from the
deepest impression of his own summer woods" (569). The prospect
of shared travel experience, as the boy gives hope to the man, is
portrayed in verses from Wordsworth's "Michael" when Uncle
Stephen feels that "objects which he had loved before were dearer
now. From the boy there came feelings and emanations—things
that were light to the sun and music to the wind: and the old man's
heart seemed born again" (572).

Uncle Stephen, like Robert Nathan's *Portrait of Jenny*, is an experiment in time traveling, for the mind is able to project itself into
both past and future. In each case, the method implies a dissatisfaction with a present that limits personal freedom. On a psychological
level, Reid is playing upon the relationship of desire to will as it is
used in mental telepathy and in thought transference. His approach
shows considerable originality insofar as Tom projects his desires to

Uncle Stephen at the same time that Uncle Stepehn is thinking about Tom. Hence the two worlds of psychic energy meet and become one present in which both characters achieve the happiness each seeks through their relationship to each other.

The emotion that Reid treats in *Uncle Stephen* within the dream is similar to that portrayed in *The Garden God* except that it is more sensuous in its lyrical movement. The strange and haunting beauty of this story is achieved through Reid's quiet prose style. As F. M. Godfrey noted about Reid's style "A fine sense of humour pervades his descriptive passages and his human situations, and his sympathetic mind embraces the natural beauty of man and beast, of river and thicket and above all of the sea."[18] Russell Burlingham states that, in the revised text of *Uncle Stephen* in the passage where Tom fixes his attention on the butterfly, the relative pronoun *who* replaces the earlier *that*. Such an emendation points up Reid's tendency to humanize the lower forms of life, for Reid "would no more have deprived a butterfly of its identity than a human being."[19] When commenting about *Uncle Stephen*, F. M. Godfrey notes that Reid "derived from the Greeks his close affinity to nature, a gentle paganism, an absorbing pantheism. There were hours when he could 'pass *into* nature', when he seemed to lose consciousness of any separate existence. . . ."[20] An anonymous reviewer in the *Times Literary Supplement* commented: "Mr. Reid seems to deepen our sense of consciousness and to bring us for a while into a fairer world of marvelous intuitions."[21] In a chapter—"Intimations of Immortality"—which discusses Alain-Fournier, Proust, and Forrest Reid, Robert Liddell describes *Uncle Stephen* as "that lovely fusion of the old man's vision and the young man's dream which could not fail to reach a part of its true public—though it cannot yet have found its way to many who might greatly love and admire it."[22]

III   Brian Westby

When Reid wrote *Brian Westby* (1934), he abandoned the dream technique of *Uncle Stephen* for Romantic Realism. A self-portrait of the artist as an unfulfilled visionary, this novel is both a novelist's novel and a spiritual autobiography. The quotation on the title page from the unknown writer "Yakovnin" describes the tension between the demands of art and life. "But sometimes," Yakovnin writes, "the problem is more difficult of solution, when the voice of duty seems to call in opposite directions, and sympathy and inclination them-

selves are divided. In such cases it is well to consider the claims of
the past, for that at least is known, like an old friend; whereas the
present is still untried, and the future may be an illusion."[23] Dedicated to Stephen Gilbert, Reid's literary executor, friend, and an
imaginative novelist from Belfast, the dedication is a testament of
the master to the creativity of his student. When Gilbert wrote his
first novel, *The Landslide*, a fantasy, he dedicated it to Forrest Reid
as a tribute from his "friend and pupil."[24]

The background of *Brian Westby* is a summer resort at Ballycastle
to which Martin Linton, a middle-aged novelist, returns after twenty years to recuperate from an illness. Although he has achieved
success as a writer, his marriage to Stella had failed because of
religious differences; and he feels lonely and unfulfilled until he
discovers the adolescent Brian Westby whose personal beauty
seems to give him a new lease on life; for, since Brian is writing a
novel, Linton offers to be of assistance. During their conversations,
Linton realizes that Brian is his son, that Stella has remarried, and
that Brian is now torn between his father and mother. When Brian
breaks his promise to go away with Linton, the story reaches its
climax. Without a note of explanation from Brian, Martin Linton is
left waiting at the hotel; and, as the novel ends, he sinks back into
his former loneliness, caught in the ebb tide of his life. The theme of
the story is the growth of friendship between father and son, and
their development is sensitively portrayed in a lyrical mode. The
portrait of Brian Westby as a shy, creative youth who is growing up
in a world where adult values often tear adolescents apart is a stroke
of genius.

When Linton discovers Brian sitting in a hollow between the sand
dunes and the sea, and reading Linton's novel *Hippolytus*, he is so
struck by the nobility of the boy's Irish features that a deep un-
tapped reservoir of feeling surges into his consciousness (24). As
they discuss *Hippolytus* and creative writing in general, their
spiritual kinship begins and develops; and it causes Brian to understand his father through the style of his book. Because Brian's writing tends toward Realism, Linton attempts to explain the importance of the imaginative mode, the use of myth, and the necessity of
an ideal in visions of reality. If Brian would read Linton's books in
sequential order, he would see the ideal "naked and complete."
Reid's use of imagery to describe the way Martin Linton sees Brian
reveals the mythopoeic imagination in process. At first Brian's

beauty seems as natural and impersonal as "the beauty of sea and sky and shore" (27); but, translated into a mythical mode, he becomes like the "young men on the Parthenon frieze, riding by in proud humility." The youth then reminds Linton of "the world . . ., the spirit . . ., the beauty he loved best" (27), "a bit of that ancient world" that he tried to portray in his novels. To Stella, however, Linton's books were "definitely and aggressively anti-Christian"; but they disguised "their true teaching under a kind of beauty" (184). Their influence she considered dangerous because "the whole aim and purpose . . . was to extol and inculcate a kind of paganism—Pantheism he would call it" (184).

Although Linton no longer believes in Presbyterianism, he follows Brian to church on Sunday where, by means of an interior monologue, he analyzes the process by which he became a nature worshipper. For him, belief in an ideal is "a prayer"; to remain "constant to it is a faith" (190). In and through nature, he found peace; in the Greek ideal of beauty, goodness, and spirituality, he found esthetic truth. Happy in the service of an ideal which has made his life meaningful, he prays to "the unknown God" that he may communicate the beauty discovered in life and art to readers who are willing to accept spiritual values. The irony and pathos of the story is revealed when Brian walks out of Linton's life as Stella had done earlier, for Linton faces the future alone once again.

The dramatic tension underlying this novel centers around Stella's Christianity and Linton's Humanism which led to their divorce, but their incompatibility of temperament and their different lifestyles were even more basic. When Brian insists that Linton confront Stella, he reopens old wounds; but he also suffers, since the alternative his mother offers places the burden of choice on Brian. The interior conflict then becomes the boy's honor, since he is forced to choose between his mother who had reared him without help, and his father who had just appeared on the scene with his offer of an attractive future. In the concluding pages of the novel, the effect of Brian's departure on Linton, which Reid portrays with deep sensitivity and feeling, is one of the most poignant passages in the book.

To establish and to contrast Christian and Greek values, Reid uses Linton's novel *Hippolytus* as the controlling image of his own novel. From the moment Linton's book is published, Stella's aversion to her husband increases until he finally agrees to a divorce. Unknown to him, Brian was born, Stella remarried, and the son's name was Westby. Throughout the novel, Reid makes Linton vastly superior to Stella by virtue of his mind and his spiritual vision, which contrast with her limited provincial attitude toward life which is associated with her religious beliefs. The conflict between paganism and Christianity begins in the opening pages when Linton is described as a writer whose primary concern is to capture the stream of beauty around him, a purpose that continues throughout Reid's novel.

When Linton discusses with Brian the process of writing a novel, he imagines the opening lines of Brian's manuscript to be similar in tone to the speeches of Socrates to Phaidros (30). When he reads the manuscript, however, Brian's work is more like Samuel Butler's *The Way of All Flesh*, less like "the Parthenon frieze," and far from the spiritual "symbols" of Linton's own writings. As their friendship grows, Linton explains the concept of a "spiritual affinity which existed below the wide difference of age and experience" (104). Linton's hopes for a future with Brian are built on threads of poetry and music that make the possibility "mysteriously lovely and intimate, as if they had known each other for years" (104). Against the background of the sea, the ebb and flow of Linton's feelings are as primitive as they are poetic. When Brian discovers that his father offers him a more meaningful life beyond Ballycastle, his moodiness increases in intensity since they communicate on different wave lengths. What Linton foresaw and desired was a relationship of reason, one like that of master to pupil as it had been in the Italian Renaissance; but Brian is emotionally involved. Although their discussions about art continue as Linton instructs his eager listener in his esthetics of "art as vision" portrayed through a temperament, rather than as "life in the raw," they are really world's apart. When Linton explains the difference between his vision of life and that of the boy's mother—the dichotomy between Christianity and the Greek world view—Brian is not an immediate convert.

Although the device of a novel's being written within a novel is functional, it is the rather obvious means by which Reid defends his own devotion to the Greek ideal and to Humanism as a way of life. Bonamy Dobrée criticized Reid for his failure to use words to evoke "the reality of actual life."[25] True as this criticism may be, Reid does succeed in portraying the lyrical flow of feeling and the pathos that is basic to the mood of Romantic melancholy that the novel evokes.

Russell Burlingham has selected several passages from this novel to illustrate Reid's style and his use of the epiphany technique.[26] The scene in which Linton waits in the rain for Brian's decision to go with him or to stay with his mother portrays a depth of feeling that is classically restrained. Since Reid's novels are not readily available, the following selection may help do him the justice he so assuredly deserves. Toward the end of *Brian Westby*, Linton cautions Brian not to act lightly; and Reid's passage reveals his firm control of feeling through his positioning of dream and reality: "I'm not acting lightly, and I have considered," Brian said.

Linton was silent, and in the silence there floated before him a vision infinitely alluring. It took shape and colour in his imagination—a dream of renewed life and happiness. It grew brighter and brighter, more and more tempting—a dream of their life together—of work and of leisure, of sympathy and friendship, of shared thoughts and feelings and plans, of the long intimacy of firelit winter evenings, of summer holidays, of watching Brian's career, of helping in it, of being present when he had his first success. The dream rose before his inward gaze, like a summer-morning sun over a lonely world, filling the sky and drenching the earth with its light and warmth and blessing. And from a dream it could so easily pass into reality! There would be plenty of time later to discuss details—to plan and to settle. Plenty of time—an enchanted river, cool and fresh and clear, flowing on and on to an unknown sea. (289)

At the very end of the novel, when Linton realizes that Brian has chosen to remain with Stella, he descends the hill to the shore, to the place "where they had sat that morning making their plans. But the tide was farther out now. There was a broad strip of uncovered yellow sand between the rocks and the sea" (298).

Why *Brian Westby* has not met with a wide reading audience is difficult to explain. Although the emotional experience that it treats is perhaps limited, it is, nevertheless, a classic of its kind. For those who feel the lyrical quality and the pulse of the emotion captured, it will always be a delicately beautiful story—one haunting in a strange, inexplicable way. As a portrait of the predicament of writers, lonely, middle-aged and unfulfilled like Linton, whose search for the reality of beauty seems destined never to be realized, this novel is highly successful. The restraint, the economy of character, the time and the setting, and the control of a point of view that is internalized so that the reader sees both Brian and Linton's analysis of events are testimony to Reid's skill in the art of novel writing. Of

Brian Westby, John Boyd writes that it "is in many ways unlike Reid's other novels, though its theme—friendship—is a recurring one; it possesses a dramatic intensity seldom reached in the other novels *(Uncle Stephen* is an exception), and its sense of form profoundly satisfies the reader."[27] In comparing Forrest Reid and E. M. Forster, Russell Burlingham has noted that both "find common ground . . . in their feeling for youth, for naturalness, for innocence, as against the intolerance, the narrowness and the unimaginativeness which masquerades as 'experience.' For pretentiousness, whether in art or life, neither of them has a moment's patience."[28]

IV   The Retreat

The Retreat; or, The Machinations of Henry (1936),[29] written five years after *Uncle Stephen,* is a prelude to it although complete in itself. Since the title is taken from Henry Vaughan's poem "The Retreat," the verse prefacing the opening chapter sets the mood of the story:

> Happy those early days, when I
> Shined in my angel-infancy!
> Before I understood this place
> Appointed for my second race,
> Or taught my soul to fancy aught
> But a white, celestial thought;
> When yet I had not walked above
> A mile or two from my first Love,
> And looking back—at that short space—
> Could see a glimpse of his bright face;
> When on some gilded cloud, or flower,
> My gazing soul would dwell an hour,
> And in those weaker glories spy
> Some shadows of eternity. . . .[30]

A fable of childhood happiness and innocence that yields to the dawn of experience, this novel also resounds with echoes of William Blake and of Wordsworth. Although "some shadows of eternity" remain, time brings "a black art to dispense/ A several sin to every sense" as innocence yields to experience. Henry, Tom Barber's black cat, is both a symbol of feelings and sensations that accompany the dawn of puberty in the thirteen year old Tom and a comment on maturation.

The opening scene of *The Retreat* is "the exact transcription of a dream" that began in terror and that ended in a dream of happiness with the appearance of a lovely, graceful faun. The graveyard scene with the cats on the tombstones and the sorcery this scene suggests is based on Reid's visit to a cemetery outside Brunswick Square with E. M. Forster and his black cat. By fusing dream and reality, by portraying the world through the eyes of a yonger Tom, Reid wrote about the world of nature he loved best when "meadow, grove and stream, the earth and every common sight" had the "glory and freshness of a dream." The symbolism of the novel is a "pledge of allegiance . . . formed from the beginning with the animal world."[31]

The theme of *The Retreat* is the dawn of adolescence in the imaginative, sensitive Tom. In each of Reid's novels, as we have seen, the child is father to the man. Tom is a dreamer, walks in his sleep, believes in fairy tales, sings arias from Donizetti, collects stamps, races caterpillars, finds classroom study boring, loves bonfires, and keeps in very close touch with nature. An only child who plays with his black cat Henry, he wants a dog of his own, and also dreams of a sympathetic companion. Although Clement Pascoe is his friend, the scientific interests and experiments to which Tom half-heartedly acquiesces leave something to be desired in Tom's opinion. So intense is Tom's yearning for a friend that Gamelyn, an angel, appears to him in three visions at times of crisis. Since Tom is an exceptional boy, his individuality, like that of the artist, accounts for his difference. From his point of view, the measure of the world is taken. In contrast to his very "factual" father, to the scientific Dr. Macrory, and to Pascoe "a natural botanist," Tom stands apart by an imagination that brings naiads and undines to life. Tom is also fascinated by Henry's antics, a symbol of the black arts that Tom is coming to know.

Although Tom lives in the natural environment of Ballysheen and is at home in its natural wooded beauty, he creates a better world in his daydreams whenever the adult world limits his freedom. At the first touch of spring, his mind wanders beyond the classroom to the long summer vacation ahead. As he grows in his understanding of literature beyond the level taught by Miss Jenkins, he questions the literal truth of Bible history, and selects the more imaginative biblical stories—which, much to his mother's horror, he compares to the tales of the Arabian Nights—for his own use. Gradually, as adoles-

cence brings understanding, Tom becomes aware of a romance between Mr. Holbrook, his music teacher, and Miss Jimpson, his
homeroom teacher. During an illness, Pascoe brings Tom wine
gums that help his spirit more than his stomach. Together they read
strange tales of black and white magic, enjoy picnics in the
Glenagivney Hills, swim in the lake, and build a magnificent bonfire
that hypnotizes Tom. In one of Tom's strange adventures, the angel
Gamelyn takes him on a flight through space to Eden where Tom
speaks to the serpent. During the night, he has a dreadful nightmare in which a cat like a large black lynx is about to attack him.
Saved by a young man passing by, he learns that the dream was
"only the image" of his fear (328). In time, as Tom grows to a deeper
understanding of himself, the angel reveals his identity saying, "I
am you; the beast that is gone was you; do not think about it, but go
to sleep" (329).

With an animist's feeling for nature, Tom has a naturalist's love of
animals, fish, and insects with whom he wishes to be friends. He is
horrified to realize that birds subsist on worms and that aggression
repeats itself in ruthless vengeance on inferior life forms. He has a
vegetarian's attitude toward meat, and a pacifist's abhorrence of
violence. In the natural harmony and beauty of Glenagivney countryside with its sea, its hills, and its clouds, he is completely at home
in a world "only remotely related to this world."

Stretched out on the purple heather as Tom listens to the turf-
cutters talking, his search for meaning behind scriptural stories becomes a virtual garden of Eden before the Fall: "Pascoe had produced a pocket-lens and with his penknife was performing some
kind of botanical dissection; Chrysanthemum was searching for rab-
bits; Blossom and Welcome continued to nose about for provender;
while Kerrigan and the turf-cutters smoked and pursued a desultory
conversation interlarded with humorous yarns. Everyone was doing
exactly what he wanted to do, Tom reflected, and not interfering
with anybody else; and this seemed to him to be exactly the way life
ought to be conducted" (273).

Since Tom cannot imagine a world better than a community of
nature, nor understand the biblical garden of Eden (although Pascoe
had sketched its physical dimensions for him), his knowledge must
come through a dream in which he is transported to Eden. Riding
on the back of a hippopotamus, he sees the flowers, birds, butterflies, and bees existing in perfect harmony. From the friendly

serpent, he learns that the curse was only on Adam for eating the fruit of the Tree of Life, not on the animals and birds; that there is "no invisible world," but only "degrees of perfection in the organs of vision" (290); and that "time is an illusion" (291). When Tom closed his eyes at the serpent's suggestion, the fall from innocence is perpetuated on him: "He felt the air filling with the serpent's peculiar odour, felt the serpent's coils twining about his naked body like a climbing plant, felt the serpent's face pressing, smooth cheek by cheek, against his own. There was a minute of dizziness—a blank" (291).

The fear of sexual encounter is repeated in another dream that grows from the first, and the second takes place in a large bare stone room with black draperies in which a wizard and his black cat practice the black arts while Tom is held prisoner. As he tries to escape, the black cat tears at his doublet trying to reach his throat. When he awakes, he is back in his room in the Fort Hotel; and Pascoe is trying to rouse him from his deep sleep.

From Danny McCoy, the old sea dog who had been "away" in his youth, Tom learns that strange things happen at Port-a-Doris. In fact, Danny has seen two figures on the battlement in night clothes, and the big one in his "pelt" has a "shining around him . . . looking like the angel of God" (296). Tom never told either Pascoe or Danny about his dreams. Before the summer holiday ends, Henry is joined by six other cats and no longer wants to be petted. Caught in a rain storm, Tom hides in the graveyard bushes; and the dream of the stone house with the wizard and the black cat as large as a lynx and as threatening returns, just as Gamelyn in the form of a young man with a dog appears again on the scene and allays Tom's fears. After the all too short vacation is over, Tom is thinking about visiting Uncle Stephen Collet, who, like mother, is Tom's type of person.

The Retreat is one of Reid's most successful studies of the dawning of adolescence in a sensitive, imaginative boy. By the use of fantasy, Reid shapes the process of growing up as he captures the thoughts and desires in Tom's mind with magnificent ease. While *The Retreat* does not have the passion or intensity of *Uncle Stephen,* it reflects a deep insight into the emotions of a child who has a natural sense of the marvelous; but what is revealed is not so important as what emerges obliquely. The black arts of which Henry the cat is the functioning symbol convey imaginatively the impression of worldly temptations that invade the territory of innocence; and each of the three appearances of the angel Gamelyn marks a phase of growth and struggle within Tom's soul.

Not only does this novel achieve a high point in its symbolism, it also marks a definite advance in Reid's narrative style. The simplicity, directness, and lucidity of his prose, his economy of phrase, and his concreteness in description reveal the Greek ideal of style toward which he continually strove. By virtue of this novel, Reid deserves to rank among important English prose stylists. As Edwin Muir observed: "This is an original and exquisite piece of work, full of the most delightful surprises, yet always true and just, and executed with consummate skill."[32] Moreover, Edward Crankshaw, writing in *Time and Tide*, commented: "I have never read a truer thing than this story and I never shall. It is an extraordinary achievement."[33]

V   Young Tom

With a quotation from Milton's *Paradise Lost*, Reid introduces the last book in his trilogy, *Young Tom; or, Very Mixed Company* (1944),[34] a portrait of Tom Barber at age ten:

> What call'st thou solitude? Is not the Earth
> With various living creatures, and the Air,
> Replenished, and all these at thy command
> To come and play before thee? Knowest thou not
> Their language and their ways? . . . With these
> Find pastime.

The theme of the three novels in the *Tom Barber* trilogy is the search for a faithful friend who will stand the test of time. Because of the absence of a plot in *Young Tom*, the action is built with a succession of adventures both remarkable and ordinary that Tom experiences in his relationship to grownups, animals, and friends. As a lonely child he talks to his dogs Barker, Roger, and Pincher, who accompany him in his rambles along the river and throughout the countryside of Belfast and Tramore. A naturalist from the start, he wins two books in Sunday School that advance his interests: *Nat the Naturalist* by George Manville Fenn, and *The Curiosities of Natural History* by Frank Buckland, which he prefers by far to "Lays of Ancient Rome" by Thomas B. Macaulay.

The imaginative Tom is in constant conflict with his father, whose disbelief in nymphs and undines is well known. Although his mother shares his faith in the existence of spirits, she can never convince either her husband or Dr. Macrory, the medical doctor who loves Greek and archaeology, of her intuitions. To Miss Sabine, his Sunday School teacher, Tom relates well; to her daughter Althea, "a giggler and a tease," he gives toleration; for Max Sabine, he harbors fears of treachery. With his botanist friend Pascoe, Tom builds an aquarium or sails a small boat on the river in the everyday world. In Tom's fantasy the church bells—to the intoxicating rhythm of Poe's "The Bells"—become a huge bat, and a face with a pointed cap peers down at him. A memorial window in the church to Ralph Seaford who died at the age of ten anchors in Tom's subconscious thoughts; and, when Tom learns that his grandmother's house was formerly the Seaford residence, Ralph Seaford "visits" him at night, a fact corroborated by the superstitious Irish maid Phemie.

The wish for a companion like Ralph Seaford is realized in Tom's discovery of James-Arthur, a sixteen year old farm boy who, in rescuing Tom's boat from deep water, becomes his friend. As young Arthur strips to swim, he looked to Tom like a "butterfly" emerging from a chrysalis, or like a god with fair hair and a bronzed body. He becomes "part of the natural scene, like the grass and the trees and the river and the sky, and the dragonfly asleep upon his water lily" (38). When Tom compliments him, James-Arthur only smiles and says that Tom is a "queer wee lad," though "it was easy to see that secretly he was not displeased" (38). When Tom is with James-Arthur, he is completely happy; alone, his existential sadness returns with its heartache. Though the friendship is mutual, James-Arthur is sufficiently mature to balance Tom's sentimentalism. James-Arthur associates with girls as well as boys much to Tom's surprise. Would "chums" be the proper word to describe the relationship of James-Arthur to him, Tom wonders. When Mother sings Tom's favorite love songs just before bedtime, the romantic lyrics reenforce his deepest feelings: "I think of all thou art to me/ I dream of what thou canst not be"; or, in the words from Arthur Sullivan's "My Dearest Heart,"

> All the dreaming is broken through,
> Both what is done and undone I rue,
> Nothing is steadfast, nothing is true,

> But your love for me and my love for you,
> My dearest, dearest heart. (45)

But the lyrics to "When Sparrows Build" capture for Tom the birth of romance:

> . . . .
> O my lost love, and my own, own love,
>   And my love that loved me so!
> Is there never a chink in the world above
>   Where they listen to words from below?
> Nay, I spoke once, and I grieved thee sore,
>   I remember all that I said,
> And now thou wilt hear me no more—no more
>   Till the sea gives up her dead. (46)

If Tom's days are filled with excitement, his dreams at night take sinister and ghostly shapes. In one nightmare, he is chased up the steps of a tower by a winged female form from whom escape seems impossible; but, though her hold is finally broken as the dreamer kicks her down to labyrinthine depths, her finger, spun out like a thin spider's web, still adheres to him. When Tom explains his dream to his mother, she tells him not to look at Granny's Japanese prints before bedtime. In Granny's house at Tramore with its beautiful garden setting, a boy of his own age in a blue jersey and shorts appears like a vision of the boy Ralph Seaford. While Tom leafs through copies of old *Graphics*, the boy stands with his hands on Tom's shoulder, thereby causing his loneliness to disappear (68). At home, Phemie reports that Mary Donaghy, the maid, saw a ghost of a little boy in Master Tom's room.

Dr. Macrory quotes Milton's *Comus* to support the existence of spirits: " 'Millions of spiritual creatures walk the earth unseen, both when we wake and when we sleep' " (73). To his mother, however, a belief in ghosts is merely a certain type of Irish superstition. Since Tom, like William Blake, the English romantic visionary poet, has the ability to control the supernatural, he tells Ralph to stay in his own house at Tramore. Meanwhile, Tom's life in nature is a continual hymn to joy in an eternal summer until Max Sabine kills his pet squirrel, Edward. As he flings Sabine's gun into the river in anger, Tom knows that nothing can ever bring Edward back; for the world of manmade evil has changed the balance of nature.

The philosophical framework of *Young Tom*, like each of Reid's other novels, is controlled by a Greek world view of custom, belief, and animism; and the view is revealed through a series of images that express the author's vision of life. By making Tom a precocious boy whose feeling for nature is animistic, and by endowing him with a mythopoeic imagination, Reid achieves a unique fusion of realism and romanticism. From the opening chapter to the conclusion, Tom's natural, spontaneous, uninhibited response to the life force in nature is a threnody to earth in which reverence for the spirit of all living things plays an integral part. In Chapter I, as Tom watches the dour William working in the garden, he

could imagine some thoughtless young green shoot, filled with an ardent zest of life, wriggling excitedly up through the brown soil, catching one glimpse of William's sour countenance, and hastily retreating underground again.

The strange thing was that nothing of the kind happened. If anywhere, it was in Tom's own private garden that plants exhibited signs of nervousness. The struggle for life there was bitter in the extreme, and not a few had given it up as hopeless, while the survivors hung limp and melancholy heads. Turning to this questionable oasis now, he could not help feeling that last night's attentions had only increased its resemblance to a violated grave, and he stooped to pull out a weed, and to press down the earth round a recently transplanted orange lily. (13–14)

In the throbbing life of the natural world, Tom hears "the myriad voices of Nature . . . calling—whispering in the trees that overhung and cast deep pools of shadow on the sunlit road—calling more loudly and imperatively from bird and beast and insect. Everywhere was life and the eager joy of life. The very air seemed alive, and from the earth a living strength was pushing upwards and outwards—visible in each separate blade of grass and delicate meadow flower no less than in the great chestnut-tree standing at the corner where the road turned" (16–17).

Tom's imagination, like that of his author, is nourished first on the four volume edition of *Nat the Naturalist*, and then on *The Library* of Apollodorus and Frazer's *Golden Bough*, which are lent to Tom by Dr. Macrory who encourages him to study Greek language and literature. For, "though separated in time by nearly two thousand years, he and the Greek mythologist became collaborators" (123). Dr. Macrory also encourages Tom to study natural history because, "like the Greeks, you're fond of animals—which is a spiritual quality and has nothing whatever to do with science" (57). When Tom wants to read Uncle Stephen's book on archaeology and natural history to learn about Orpheus, Dr. Macrory informs him that Hermes is its spiritual center.

Everywhere in nature Tom invests the lowliest forms of life with sentience and personality. The bumble bee is a "good-natured person"; the beetle, affectionate; and the mouse has a family to whom he would tell the tale of his adventures. The smallest ant knows what to do in an emergency, frogs spawn in the pond where they were born as tadpoles, and every year the swallows return home. In school, Miss Sabine explains the process of birds and insects as instinctive or as inherited memory, but Tom remembers that "she had been unable to tell him why swallows had inherited a memory so good that it could guide them all the way from Egypt to the exact spot in Ballysheen where their nests were. He didn't believe that it was memory at all. Mother's view that they had simply been created by God with a special gift, seemed far more satisfactory, though it didn't explain how the gift worked . . ." (89–90).

The Greek world also attracts Tom's dogs, who engage in choral singing at Tom's instigation, intoning "a religious hymn to some invisible spirit—universal Pan" (94). As Tom lies in the shade of an ancient oak on the river bank, the sound of the huge water wheel with its tranquilizing effect sends his imagination on flights of fancy. In his fantasy, "it became a living and benevolent monster, guardian of the river and of this green shade." He wonders why animals— "even fabulous and imaginary ones—" were "so much closer to him than human beings" (103).

From Tom's observation of nature, he concludes that the great earth mother has no favorites since it is rather impartial; "a hippopotamus, a blackbird, and a boy were equally pleasing to her, equally provided for, equally her sons" (112). His father explains that Tom's idea of equality is based on "an ethical conception of the greater democracy. . . . It means, . . . a social community in which you and I and Tom, and squirrels and hedgehogs and dogs and mice, all have precisely equal rights to freedom and happiness—the communist ideal, in short; with this important difference, that it is to be extended to the non-human races. . . . Therefore, no more animal circuses and shows; no more shutting up in zoos; and if we are to be absolutely consistent, I'm afraid no more . . ." (113). To Tom, his father's message means the end of his aquarium.

When Max shoots Tom's pet squirrel Edward, the world's trap for the unwary is a repetition of the Glaucus myth he is reading. In Tom's mind a vision of a better world takes shape where violence is no more. With all the vividness of an earthly paradise, he saw

a wide curving beach of yellow sand where children were playing in the sunlight at the edge of a timeless sea. They were building castles on the sand, and their happy voices reached him—gay, innocent, laughing. Vision or memory, the scene brought with it no feeling of strangeness, only the sense of returning to a lovely and familiar place, which would always be there, though at times it might be hidden from him. . . . That happy shore he knew—and it was drawing closer, it seemed very near, already less dream than reality. (154–55)

The novel ends in an evocation of the "golden isles" as the desired landscape of Tom and Forrest Reid's ideal world.

Reid's literary genius was finally recognized in 1944 when he was awarded the James Tait Black Memorial Prize for *Young Tom*. There is no doubt that this novel is in the classic tradition of books about boys. No character previously portrayed by Reid has Tom's naturalness, normality, and closeness to earth. Not only has Reid drawn Tom artistically, but the language of the novel is excellent English prose that is conversational in quality and that has the rhythm of human speech. Because the action of the story is narrated completely through Tom's consciousness, its effect is complete verisimilitude.

Each character in the book is lifelike, including the dogs and the mixed animal friends of Tom's world. Tom's mother is drawn with complete sympathy and understanding, which is most unusual for Reid. His father, by contrast, symbolizes the rational, scientific point of view; and he is bound to conflict with the more imaginative Tom but in a humorous, genial way. Miss Jimpson's attraction to the music master, Mr. Holbrook, is sensitively portrayed, as is Tom's gradual realization of their relationship. Granny—her garden at Tramore, her Oriental prints and china, her complete independence in her own world—and Phemie and Mary, the maids who are superstitious to the core, are homespun yet completely credible.

The gardener William, too, with his natural grouchiness, his green thumb, and his magic pipe that never needs refilling, is a touch of the earth itself. Doctor Macrory, the good-natured bachelor, with his love for Greek and his admiration for Tom; the young Pascoe, amateur botanist; and his lovely aunt whom Tom admires are very human characters, imaginatively conceived and realistically portrayed. The strength of Miss Sabine's character, the meanness of Max, and the laughter of Althea, although not dwelt on in any detail, are the materials of which life is made, and Reid makes the reader feel their humanness. Even Ralph Seaford actually appears to the reader as he appeared to Tom or Phemie because his presence is so convincingly suggested. The individuality of each portrait is created because of Reid's great care with minute detail.

In *Young Tom*, Reid has achieved the directness and the simplicity that were evident in *Brian Westby* and in *The Retreat*. No word is superfluous, no scene extraneous; there is magnificent economy visible throughout. He has cleverly managed his episodic narrative so that Tom's character develops in relation to the pattern of his experiences. Each chapter closes with such finesse and expert craftmanship that the reader anticipates each new adventure. Although Tom's world is built of both dream and reality, each is so artistically fused that the two worlds become one. Since this world is also a garden, Reid re-creates the natural beauty of the countryside of Northern Ireland as the harmonious background for Tom's adventures.

Reid's books on boyhood and adolescence, the aspects of life that he knew and loved best, achieve a depth and a richness because he imaginatively lived each novel as he wrote it. Like other great works of the imagination, the *Tom Barber* series gives to the reader whatever he is capable of deriving from it. As Tom grows up and sees the world in relation to good and evil, the reader becomes aware that each story brings a deeper understanding of the problems of human life although they have been envisioned through the experiences of a sensitive boy. As Laura Benet noted, "the penetrating quality of Forrest Reid's genius is best revealed by the way in which daily events glide into the realm of the supernatural."[35]

It is difficult to understand why Virginia Woolf objected to the *Tom Barber* series since both writers were concerned with the problem of time, with interior states of feeling, and with the same humane values. E. M. Forster writes: "I remember Virginia Woolf's giving him a trial and turning him down."[36] Jessamyn West comes closest to explaining Mrs. Woolf's myopia when she says that it was perhaps because "Tom, like his creator, 'was not interested in maturity.' "[37] In her judgment, Reid belongs "in the great tradition of books about boys."[38] Like Jessamyn West, Edwin Muir complimented Reid's ability to create boys; for Muir wrote that *Young Tom*, like *The Retreat* and *Uncle Stephen*, "has a radiant lucidity, a crystalline serenity which seems to maintain intact the very essence of childhood. Mr. Reid is an original writer, but his originality is easily overlooked because there is in it not a single touch of violence, or even of emphasis. His three books about the childhood of Tom will probably remain as one of the most original and most perfect works of imagination of his time."[39]

CHAPTER 6

Conclusion

THE art and the achievement of Forrest Reid reveal him to be an
Anglo-Irish visionary writer from Belfast whose reputation as
an English prose stylist, an important psychological novelist, and a
critic of some distinction, should establish his place in literary history. The pattern of his stylistic development and the growth of his
fictional technique from *The Kingdom of Twilight* and *The Garden
God* to the *Young Tom* trilogy and the posthumous *Denis Bracknel*
demonstrate a progression in economy, restraint, lucidity, and
radiance that characterize his best works. Integral to his style is a
natural, rhythmic cadence related to his rich Celtic inheritance. His
feeling for nature, similar in its sensitivity to Wordsworth's
animism, colors each landscape that he portrays in contrasting images of light and darkness. He also captures the physical sense of the
place, whether in Ballyreagh, Carrick-a-rede, Bruges, Eleusis, or
Belfast, to create an illusion of reality. Both atmosphere and geography, then, serve to contrast city and country, outer and inner,
time and timelessness. The search for a divine friend, the longing
for an Eden from which each of us is exiled, so lyrically orchestrated
in his haunting autobiography *Apostate*, and to a lesser extent in
Private Road, are themes that possessed him throughout his life and
served his narrative purposes well.

In each period of Reid's stylistic growth, the theme of youth and
youthful friendships in either boyhood or adolescence controls his
narrative, which is confessional to a greater or lesser degree according to the needs of his story. Since he portrays his action through the
mind of a child who is also a dreamer, and maintains his point of
view through the child's consciousness at the child's own level of
perception, his subtle explorations of feeling and unusual states of
mind whether awake or in dream, are exceptional attributes of his
technique and of his style. He also connects cosmic loneliness to

144

homesickness as the overarching metaphor that sets parameters on his heroes' quest for meaning, truth, and permanence, a quest that is identical to his own intellectual search for a country of the mind and heart in which to find peace. Although Reid always used Greek allusions functionally, if somewhat self-consciously at first, once he discovered Greece as the integrating symbol of his life and art, he gained a unified perspective from which he never deviated.

From the publication of *Apostate* in 1926, the style of each succeeding novel from *Demophon* in 1927 to *Denis Bracknel* in 1947 gained in directness, simplicity, and beauty. Just as he used animism to support his vision of life, he used the friendship theme to structure his cry for freedom and for unity. Since the spirit of youth and its vision were predominant values to Reid as a writer, he used dreams and dream psychology to make his vision prevail. The geography of the dream and its Utopian content are skillful devices employed to establish the humane values that he asserts. Nonviolence, freedom to be oneself, peace, harmony, happiness, and friendship are life-affirming values that radiate from his pages. Reid's best novels in the tradition of the modern psychological novel of boyhood and adolescence include: *Peter Waring*, (originally entitled *Following Darkness*), *The Spring Song*, *Demophon: A Traveller's Tale*, *Brian Westby*, *The Retreat*, *Young Tom*, and *Denis Bracknel*. His portrayal of boyhood friendships and fears, the change from childhood to adolescence with its complex emotional disturbances accompanying maturation, are significant contributions to twentieth century fiction.

In criticism, we have already seen Reid's success in eliciting music, poetry, and resonance from Yeats's and de la Mare's imaginative works which contain a dimension of otherworldliness inexplicable on rational grounds. By his emphasis on the importance of metaphor and music, and the lack thereof in some literary works, this standard for qualitative measurement is basic to his judgment. Readers may ask whether Reid's insistence on metaphor and music in some instances limited his judgment. Just as one may question whether his continous preoccupation with "imaginative suggestiveness," "spiritual adventures," or the search for the "beloved phantom" of youthful dreams mitigated against a so-called "objective" evaluation of literature. Certainly his critical essays on "Emily Brontë," "Seumas O'Kelley," "Arthur Lyon Raile," "Olive Schreiner," and others in *Retrospective Adventures* show Reid's unbroken absorption with states of mind and feeling as well as with spiritual dimensions of meaning. Did Reid's criterion of subjective Realism for both poetry and prose warp his judgment of literary works that fall outside his range of sympathy, and was he, at times, too close to his subject to achieve "objectivity?" Mr. Burlingham finds that his close friendship with de la Mare tended to cloud his estimate. It seems to this writer that, precisely because of his method, Reid has opened up layers of meaning that could not have been otherwise revealed.

The question of assessing a writer's biases is far too complex to be treated here, perception and values being what they are. In the case of William Dean Howells, whom Reid measured against European masters like Turgenev, Conrad, and Flaubert, he found him lacking in imaginative Realism because of an "outward fidelity" to everyday life. Yet Reid praised his art in *The Rise of Silas Lapham*, *The Kentons*, and his characterization of the boy in *The Minister's Charge*. Although Reid's judgment is balanced, Edward Wagenknecht, the eminent American critic and psychographer, has portrayed Howells with greater insight and sympathy.[1] Reid's method at times is inadequate to his judgment of George Moore, Arthur Rimbaud, and Virginia Woolf's *Jacob's Room*. Although he praised her originality, he confessed that he missed the pattern in this work, a statement that is ironical, since Woolf's technique is quite similar to his own. That she missed his originality in *Young Tom* need not be labored. When, at other times, Reid insisted that in poetry sound was sometimes more important than sense, the reader recognizes the knot into which he has tied himself, but he knew it too. What is gracious about him is that he readily admits his myopia, if we may call it such. In confessing the limitations of his "King Charles's head," he acknowledged that he could write about boys, but not about girls, since his experience and his sympathy were unequal to the task. However, what he calls his limitations translates as his range, which is quite another matter, since his range is the source of his genius and of his strength no less than his subjectivity.

Even when Reid writes about Shakespeare in *Notes and Impressions*, the lyrical genius of that great dramatist in *Twelfth Night*, *A Midsummer-Night's Dream*, and *The Tempest* is linked to the tradition of romance, and his lyrical qualities carefully indicated for the reader's appreciation. One would somehow expect Reid to write about Caliban, Prospero's slave in *The Tempest*. In "A Note on Caliban," he sympathetically defends Shakespeare's portrayal of "this creature of the woods," whose dignity and pathos have been unduly "neglected by critics." Reid's essay is so provocative that the reader hastens to return to this strange, unusual character to whom Shakespeare has given some of his greatest lines.

If *Illustrators of the Sixties* is "the definitive work" on "one phase, albeit a minor one, of nineteenth-century English art," as Mr. Burlingham claims,[2] one would never know it from Reid, who modestly called his authoritative study the "chronicle of a hobby." A treasure trove of wood engravings selected by Reid, which includes Arthur Hughes's illustrations for George Macdonald's fantasies, *At the Back of the North Wind, Dealing with Fairies*, and *The Princess and the Goblin*, causes one to marvel at the artists in this collection. It is not surprising to discover that Hughes's treatment of innocence and childhood corresponds in theme, tone, and mood to Reid's own works. Besides Dante Gabriel Rossetti, Charles Keene, and many others, Reid selects Stephen Gooden's bookplates from biblical and Classical sources, produced for the Nonesuch press, as representative of Gooden's art and of his own preferences. Among these are: "Tobit," whom we met in *The Spring Song*;[3] "Adam and Eve," and particularly the pensive young "David," standing over the fallen Goliath;[4] "a charioteer driving," and a "young athlete running,"[5] which Reid describes as "exquisite as old Greek coins."[6] In his commentary, writer links to engraver as one art comments on and interprets the other when the theme is the "appreciation of youth." In Gooden's plates for George Moore's *The Brook Kerith*, "Master and Pupil" and "Jesus Meets Paul" are illustrative of Gooden's art and genius, and of Reid's impeccable taste. In art and in literature Reid's stress is always on the beautiful.

If Reid protests that technical innovation in literature is of secondary importance to the creation of beauty and interest, we can readily understand his emphasis. Since he was very much concerned with form in painting, sculpture, and engraving, he could hardly value it less in literature. It was not that he valued technical innovation less, however, but that he valued individuality, the lyric note, and subjective Realism more. The criterion of subjective Realism gave him a method for distinguishing lesser works from greater, according to the spirit moving through language, when the word becomes flesh to communicate a "sense of something beyond."

To judge both American and European writers he always applied a qualitative test to measure imaginative intensity.

Where imaginative literature is concerned it is difficult to fault his judgment. Certainly Reid correctly assessed the imaginative qualities of the early Yeats, Walter de la Mare, W. H. Hudson, Emily Brontë, Joseph Conrad, Knut Hamsun, Olive Schreiner, Katherine Mansfield, Henry James, Maxim Gorky, and others too numerous to mention. It is not that he avoided calling attention to technical errors or blunders when he saw them, as he saw them in Howells, but rather he believed that the critic's function was appreciation of the art of storytelling and the mind behind the work. Like Virginia Woolf, he had little respect for "commercial novels," that "dreadful British Industry" that included Arnold Bennett. Fantasy and "enchanted landscapes" he valued most highly, together with certain Russian novelists; Maxim Gorky's early autobiography, *My Childhood* (1913), Reid said, was a "spiritual experience" because it portrayed the "life of the soul." In particular, Knut Hamsun's *The Wanderer*, translated by W. Worcester (1920), contained the lyrical element that Reid regarded more highly than the "diagrammed form" Henry James had used for *The Awkward Age*. Although he was James's most ardent disciple, and gave his highest praise to "the novels and tales of his maturity," calling them "unique not only in English but in European literature,"[7] Reid believed that form was organic like a tree, the "outer shell" for the "spirit dwelling within," rather than mechanically designed to the specifications of a blueprint. Because he was annoyed at critics who failed to see the genius of Hamsun, Reid wrote with considerable irritation: "One grows a little tired of the well-made book with every event in its proper place, with all the machinery competently ticking, and all the well-oiled wheels elaborately connected with all the others, so that nobody dare give a penny to a beggar, unless the beggar, out of gratitude is to save somebody's life later on."[8]

An examination of Reid's book reviews written for *The Nation and Athenaeum* clearly shows that, in the art of fiction, he valued technique very highly. A brief selection of his standards, undogmatically stated, reveal hs acuity for the art of both traditional and innovative novelists. In regard to point of view, he preferred a story to be narrated obliquely through a character's consciousness rather than to be told by an omniscient author. While he regarded Turgenev, Henry James, and Conrad as masters of the indirect method, he praised Tolstoy as a traditional novelist, and Anatole France for the "atmosphere" in his fiction, which Reid attributed to his "personality." He also believed that "a clear light of intelligence" should suffuse a creative work; that unity of tone and mood were more important than "variety of action"; and that individuality, illusion, and lyricism were necessary features of great imaginative literature. He had a keen eye for identifying the art of less well-known writers, including women, whose qualities he faithfully conveyed to the reading public in a conversational style.

As for American writers other than Henry James, Reid praised the technical innovation of Sherwood Anderson's *Winesburg, Ohio;* and the poetry in Joseph Hergerscheimer's *The Bright Shawl,* which, he said, resulted from the dynamic tie between friendship and the "sacred cause of freedom." Reid also lamented that too many American novelists were overly preoccupied with the erotic and the sexual. Although he gave high praise to Mark Twain's *Huckleberry Finn*, he thought that the Englishman Richard Jeffries' *Bevis* was "the best novel about boys ever written."[9] In William Dean Howells he found a lack of metaphor to be a stumbling block to greatness.

The greatest value for readers of Reid today lies in his humanistic vision of a better world which he structures by means of an "other" geography and by using the friendship theme. The world he depicts in dreams is peaceful, freer, and more humane than life in present society. By treating emotional relationships either in dream or by the use of myth, the subjective element connects to the universal and reaches a wider audience. Reid has integrated our modern condition of alienation, fragmentation, and loneliness within the larger framework of a Greek ethos to connect present with past time, and to point, hopefully, toward a more enlightened future. Friendship, then, is more than a theme in a relationship between persons of similar sexual nature; it is the bridge that spans continents, cultures, nations, religions, race, or sex itself. It is the means for counteracting the terrifying isolation, the universal void, the empty silence, and the impossible violence in which we live and try to be. In dream he structures peace, freedom, and nonviolence in a natural setting. His success in portraying this ideal artistically would seem to secure his place among visionary novelists. Although he distrusted relevancy as a criterion for creative art because of the implication that art was subservient to politics, he is most relevant to our need for peace and freedom in these very violent days. Reid's prophetic idealism both echoes and connects with Shelley's apocalyptic vision in *Prometheus Unbound* where, at some future time, in a new world, free from the trammels of ignorance and prejudice, persons will be

> . . . free, uncircumscribed . . .
> Equal, unclassed, tribeless, and nationless,
> Exempt from awe, worship, degree, . . . king
> Over . . . self; just, gentle, wise. . . .[10]

Such is Reid's hope, his faith, and his dream.

To modern readers, Reid's significance lies in his explorations of time, states of consciousness, and psychic phenomena; in his psychological studies of exceptional youth; and in his unending search for authenticity and humane values. To keep sane in a world of war and violence is to find a private road through which to create some semblance of order out of chaos. From *The Kingdom of Twilight* to the posthumous *Denis Bracknel*, Reid celebrates youth in the process of growing up in a world where restrictive laws limit freedom and where absurdity, materialism, and continual violence characterize daily living. His heroes reveal their author's dedication to the spirit of youth that he found in the dynamic living characters of Denis, Grif, Peter, Brian, and Tom, in whose individualism, idealism, and dreams he saw hope for the future.

Although Reid's fiction has not reached as wide a reading audience as that of Walter de la Mare or E. M. Forster, he would gain the reading public he deserves if his publishers would reissue his works. As a modern Hellenist and an English prose stylist whose novels have been recognized for their quality in international literary circles, Reid's fiction is both relevant and meaningful for the "matter of truth" that it conveys. In literary criticism, Reid has also made a significant contribution to our understanding of imaginative literature. If the function of a critic is to illuminate a text and to render an appreciation of a writer's art, craft, and truth, Reid's critical insights on the lyric, the lyrical novel, and the lyrical element in drama and in short stories are invaluable aids for modern readers and for students of literature today.

Notes and References

Chapter One

1. F. E. Breakie, "Foreword," *Forrest Reid Catalogue*, an exhibition of his books and manuscripts, Museum and National Library (Belfast, 1954).

2. Edward Wagenknecht, *Cavalcade of the English Novel* (New York, 1954), p. 568.

3. Russell Burlingham, *Forrest Reid: A Portrait and a Study* (London, 1953), p. 17.

4. Walter de la Mare, "Introduction," Burlingham, p. 10.

5. H. Montgomery Hyde, *The Love That Dared Not Speak Its Name* (Boston, 1970), pp. 2–3. On valid authority I understand that Reid was a "frustrated" rather than a practicing homosexual. His attitude toward sex reveals considerable conflict. Normal sex disgusted him; physical relationships between men he came to see as wrong; male relationships of a purely Platonic kind he sanctioned. His writings reveal a struggle to reconcile his instincts with the mores of society.

6. *Private Road* (London, 1940), p. 11. Hereafter abbreviated as PR. in this chapter.

7. *Apostate* (Boston and New York, 1926), p. 51. Intra-text references are to this work unless otherwise indicated in this chapter.

8. Russell Watson, "Ulster: The Children of Violence," *Newsweek*, April 19, 1971, pp. 46–52.

9. Information in a letter to the author from L. F. Washbrook, registrar, The Royal Belfast Academical Institution, January 19, 1959.

10. Robert Lynd, "Forrest Reid," *School News*, Royal Belfast Academical Institution, LV (Easter, 1947), 57.

11. Reuben Shapcott, ed., *The Autobiography of Mark Rutherford* [William Hale White] (London, 1936), pp. 28–29.

12. Information in a letter from D. Webster, clerk of the tutors, Christ's College, Cambridge, January 19, 1959. See also, *Biographical Register of Christ's College*, II, 886, and *Historical Register of the University of Cambridge* to the year 1910, edited by J. H. Tanner (Cambridge, 1917), p. 968.

13. Burlingham, p. 70.

14. Anthony Lewis, "Forster Homosexual Novel Due," *New York Times*, November 11, 1970, pp. 1, 46.

15. *W. B. Yeats: A Critical Study* (New York, 1915), p. 221.

16. Burlingham, pp. 18–19. See also "Forrest Reid," *The Dictionary of National Biography* 1941–50, ed. L. G. Wickham Legg and E. T. Williams (Oxford, 1959), pp. 716–17; also, "Forrest Reid," *Twentieth Century Authors*, ed. Stanley J. Kunitz and Howard Haycraft (New York, 1942), pp. 1158–59; and "Forrest Reid," *Twentieth Century Authors*, ed. Stanley J. Kunitz and Vineta Colby, 1st supp. (New York, 1955), p. 820.

17. Stephen Gilbert, "Forrest Reid—the Man," *School News*, Royal Belfast Academical Institution, LV (Easter, 1947), 55.

18. Burlingham, pp. 24, 27, 28.

19. Stephen Gwynn, *Irish Literature and Drama in the English Language* (New York, 1936), p. 206.

20. *Twentieth Century Authors* (1942), p. 1159.

21. Anne J. Richter, ed., *Literary Prizes and Their Winners* (New York, 1946), pp. 81–83. Reid's friends who had already been awarded this prize were Walter de la Mare for *Memoirs of a Midget* (1921); David Garnett, *Lady into Fox* (1922); and E. M. Forster, *A Passage to India* (1924).

22. Information in a letter from L. F. Washbrook, registrar, Royal Belfast Academical Institution, October 22, 1958.

23. Lynd, p. 57.

24. Gilbert, pp. 56–57.

Chapter Two

1. Geoffrey West, ed., "The Artist and the World Today," *Bookman* (London), LXXXVI (May, 1934), 93.

2. E. M. Forster, "Introduction," *Tom Barber* (New York, 1955), p. 7.

3. William York Tindall, *Forces in Modern British Literature* (New York, 1956), p. 146. He writes that "from 1903 onwards almost every first novel by a serious novelist was a novel of adolescence" and that each was "commonly autobiographical."

4. Cornelius Weygandt, *A Century of the English Novel* (New York, 1925), pp. 437–38.

5. S. M. Ellis, "Forrest Reid," *Bookman* (London), LVIII (May, 1920), 65–66.

6. Wilfred Stone, *The Cave and the Mountain: A Study of E. M. Forster* (Stanford, 1966), pp. 369–70.

7. Robert Liddell, "Intimations of Immortality," in *Robert Liddell on the Novel* (Chicago, 1969), p. 269.

8. Burlingham, pp. 52, 79.

9. John Sparrow, "Forrest Reid," a radio talk delivered over the Third Programme, British Broadcasting Company, February 1, 1947.

10. John Boyd, "Forrest Reid: An Introduction to His Work," *Irish Writing*, No. 4, (Cork [April, 1948]), 74.

11. "In Memoriam," *Retrospective Adventures* (London, 1941), p. 7.

12. *Retrospective Adventures*, p. 60.

13. Edward Wagenknecht, "The Little Prince Rides the White Deer: Fantasy and Symbolism in Recent Literature," *College English*, VII (May, 1946), 434, 437.

14. *Apostate*, p. 3.

15. *Ibid.*

16. Havelock Ellis, *A Study of British Genius* (Boston, 1926), p. 218.

17. *Private Road*, p. 135.

18. *Ibid.*, pp. 135–36.

19. John Zneimer, *The Literary Vision of Liam O'Flaherty* (Syracuse, 1970), p. 23.

20. *Apostate*, p. 204.

21. Matthew Arnold, "The Study of Poetry," in *Essays in Criticism*, 2nd series (London, 1903), p. 1.

22. *Private Road*, pp. 221–25.

23. John Boyd, p. 74.

24. Bernard Stern, *The Rise of Romantic Hellenism in English Literature, 1732–1786* (Menasha, Wisconsin; 1940), p. 9.

25. Among Hellenists may be mentioned such writers as Louis Ménard, Leconte de Lisle, André Chénier, Théophile Gautier, Hippolyte Taine, Catulle Mendès, Frédéric Plessis, Anatole France, and Ernest Renan. Later the French Symbolists such as Rimbaud, Verlaine, and Villiers de l'Isle-Adam interested Reid. He referred to their works whenever the Greek way of life or their ideas reinforced the reality of the spiritual values with which he was most concerned. See also, E. M. Butler, *The Tyranny of Greece over Germany* (Cambridge, Mass., 1935); and Henry Hatfield, *Aesthetic Paganism in German Literature* (Cambridge, Mass., 1964).

26. *Apostate*, p. 206.

27. *Private Road*, pp. 73–74.

28. George Seferis, [Sepheriadēs], *On the Greek Style: Selected Essays in Poetry and Hellenism*, trans. Rex Warner and Th. D. Frangopoulos (Boston, 1966), p. 123.

29. Stephen Gilbert, *Forrest Reid Memorial* (Foxton, England, 1952), pp. 11–12; rpt. in *A Library of Literary Criticism: Modern British Literature*, comp. and ed. by R. Z. Temple and M. Tucker (1966), III, 18–22.

30. Burlingham, p. 174.

31. Mary C. Bryan, "Forrest Reid and the Greek World" (Doctoral dissertation, L. C. Card No. Mic. 59-3454, Ann Arbor, Michigan: University Microfilms, 1959).

32. Philip Wheelwright, "Notes on Mythopoeia," *Sewanee Review*, LIX (Autumn, 1951), 574.

33. Frederick Clarke Prescott, *The Poetic Mind* (New York 1922), p. 54ff.

34. *Private Road*, p. 9, quoting R. W. Livingstone, *The Greek Genius and Its Meaning to Us* (London, 1924).

35. *Ibid.*, pp. 15–16.

36. Edward Wagenknecht, "As Far As Yesterday," *The Bay State Librarian*, LVI, 3 (July, 1966), 200.

37. Harold M. March, "The 'Other Landscape' of Alain-Fournier," *Publications of the Modern Language Association of America*, LVI (March, 1941), 222–79.

38. William James, *The Varieties of Religious Experience* (New York, 1902), p. 374.

39. *Apostate*, p. 206.

40. Richard Lattimore, trans., *The Odes of Pindar* (Chicago, 1947), "Pythia VI," Stanza 2, p. 74.

41. Carl G. Jung, *Psyche and Symbol*, ed. by Violet S. de Laslo (New York, 1958), p. xv.

42. *Private Road*, pp. 90–91.

43. Cyrus R. Edmonds, trans., *Cicero's Essays on Friendship and Old Age* (New York, 1922), p. 28.

44. A. J. Festugière, *Epicurus and His Gods*, trans. by C. W. Chilton from *Epicure et ses Dieux* (Cambridge, Mass., 1956), pp. 27–51.

45. *Ibid.*, p. 30.

46. *Private Road*, p. 151.

47. *Ibid.*, pp. 16–17.

48. Flyleaf following dedication of *Private Road* [n.p.]

49. Joseph Conrad, "Preface," *The Nigger of the Narcissus* (New York, 1933), xiii.

50. *Brian Westby* (London, 1934), p. 27.

51. *Apostate*, p. 27.

52. Bertram D. Lewin, *Dreams and the Uses of Regression* (New York, 1958), p. 293ff. See also, Walter de la Mare, *Behold, This Dreamer!* (New York, 1939), pp. 45, 235–36.

53. *Private Road*, pp. 221–22, 225–27, 229ff.

54. *Ibid.*, p. 236.

55. Erich Fromm, *The Forgotten Language: An Introduction to the Understanding of Dreams, Fairytales and Myths* (New York, 1951), p. 142.

56. *Apostate*, title page.

57. Theodore Ziolkowski, *The Novels of Herman Hesse: A Study in Theme and Structure* (Princeton, 1965), p. 351.

58. Kenneth Grahame (1859–1931), was an English author of fantasy and children's literature. He wrote *The Golden Age* (1895), *Dream Days* (1898), and *The Wind in the Willows* (1908), all of which are children's classics. He also compiled the *Cambridge Book of Poetry for Young Children* (1916).

59. Stone, pp. 359–60.

60. Lionel Trilling, *E. M. Forster* (New York, 1964), pp. 30–37.

61. G. D. Klingopoulos, "E. M. Forster's Sense of History: And Cavafy," *Essays in Criticism*, VIII (1958), pp. 156–65.

62. E. M. Forster, *Two Cheers for Democracy* (New York, 1951), pp. 67–76.

63. *Ibid.*, p. 73.

64. *Ibid.*, p. 67.

65. *The Milk of Paradise: Some Thoughts on Poetry* (London, 1946), p. 12.

66. *Ibid.*

67. *Ibid.*, p. 16.

68. *Ibid.*, p. 80.

69. Ralph Freedman, *The Lyrical Novel* (Princeton, 1963), p. vii.

70. *Ibid.*

71. Walter de la Mare, "Poetry in Prose" (Wharton Lecture on English Poetry, Proceedings of the British Academy, XXI, Oxford, 1935).

72. Robert Bridges, *Milton Prosody* (Oxford, England, 1921).

73. *W. B. Yeats: A Critical Study*, p. 80.

74. *Walter de la Mare: A Critical Study* (New York, 1929). Intra-text references are to this study unless otherwise indicated.

75. Freedman, p. 17.

Chapter Three

1. *The Kingdom of Twilight* (London, 1904), p. 234. Intra-text references refer to this novel unless otherwise indicated.

2. Ernest C. Dowson "Villanelle of Sunset," in *The Poetical Works of Ernest C. Dowson*, ed. Desmond Flower (London, 1934), p. 8.

> Come hither, child! and rest:
> This is the end of day,
> Behold the weary West!

3. Paul Verlaine, "Reversibilités," *Oeuvres Poétiques* (Buenos Aires, 1950), p. 101.

> Ah, dans ces mornes séjours
> Les Jamais sont les Toujours.

4. Arthur Symons, "Introduction," *The Symbolist Movement in Literature* (New York, 1958), p. vii.

5. Mario Praz, *The Romantic Agony* (New York, 1951), pp. 189–286. The vampire is one of the many themes of the "fatal woman" used by Poe, Baudelaire, D'Annunzio, and others.

6. *Private Road*, pp. 26–27.

7. *Ibid.*, p. 21.

8. *Ibid.*, p. 75.

9. Samuel, I, 14:43.

10. *The Garden God: A Tale of Two Boys* (London, 1905). Intra-text references are to this novel unless otherwise indicated.

11. Burlingham, p. 154.

12. *Apostate*, p. 76.

13. Edward Everett Hale, ed., *Selections from Walter Pater* (New York, 1901), pp. 68–84.

14. *Private Road*, pp. 66–75.

15. *Ibid.*, p. 89.

16. *The Bracknels: A Family Chronicle* (London, 1911). Intra-text references are to this novel unless otherwise indicated.

17. *Private Road*, pp. 85–86.

18. *Ibid.*, p. 89.

19. *Ibid.*

20. Anon., review, *Nation* ([London], December 9, 1911), p. 432.

21. *Denis Bracknel* (London, 1947). Intra-text references are to this novel unless otherwise indicated.

22. *Private Road*, p. 85.

23. *Ibid.*, p. 170.

24. *Ibid.*, p. 87.

25. *Following Darkness* (London, 1912). Intra-text references are to this novel unless otherwise indicated.

26. *Private Road*, pp. 120, 117.

27. William Shakespeare, "A Midsummer Night's Dream," Act. V, Sc. 1, ll. 390–94, quoted in *Following Darkness*.

28. "Alastor," Percy B. Shelley, ll. 209–211, Title page, *Following Darkness*.

29. Tindall, p. 146.

30. *Ibid.*, p. 148.

31. Burlingham, p. 79.

32. Justin O'Brien, *The Novel of Adolescence in France* (New York, 1937).

33. Thomas Mann, *Joseph and His Brothers* (New York, 1934), pp. 60–65.

34. John Milton, "Paradise Lost," ed. Merritt Y. Hughes (New York, 1957), I, ll. 254–255, p. 217.

35. *Private Road*, p. 118.

36. *Ibid.*, pp. 119–20.

37. *Ibid.*, pp. 120–21.

38. *Ibid.*, p. 121.

39. *Ibid.*, pp. 120–21.

40. Anon., review, *Times Literary Supplement* (London), October 17, 1912, p. 443B.

41. *Peter Waring* (London, 1937). Hereafter referred to as PW and FD.

42. Anon., review, *Times Literary Supplement* (London), October 17, 1912, 443B.

43. *Ibid.*, September 18, 1937, p. 673.

Chapter Four

1. *The Gentle Lover: A Comedy of Middle Age* (London, 1913). Intra-text references are to this novel unless otherwise indicated.

2. W. L. Courtney, *The Development of Maurice Maeterlinck* (London, 1904), p. 74.

3. Burlingham, pp. 88–89.

4. Courtney, *loc. cit.*

5. *Ibid.*

6. "Bruges," *Retrospective Adventures*, pp. 200–206.

7. Walter Pater, "Hippolytus Veiled," *Greek Studies* (London, 1908), pp. 152–86.

8. *Private Road*, p. 145.

9. Psalm 139: 7–10, quoted in *At the Door of the Gate* (London, 1915), title page. Intra-text references are to this novel unless otherwise indicated.

10. *Private Road*, p. 188.

11. Ernest A. Baker, *The History of the English Novel*, IX (New York, 1938), 99.

12. Anon., review, *Times Literary Supplement* (London), September 30, 1915, p. 346.

13. *Private Road*, p. 172.

14. *Ibid.*, p. 168.

15. *Ibid.*, p. 179.

16. Anon., review, New York *Times*, April 16, 1916, p. 146.

17. Anon., review, *Nation*, XVIII (October 23, 1915), 158, 160.

18. Anon., review, *Times Literary Supplement* (London), September 30, 1915, p. 346.

19. Baker. *loc. cit.*

20. *The Spring Song* (London, 1916). Intra-text references are to this novel unless otherwise indicated.

21. *Private Road*, p. 189.

22. John Donne, "Holy Sonnets," *Complete Poetry and Selected Prose of John Donne* (New York, 1941), V, 237–38.

23. *The Spring Song*, p. 1.

24. *Retrospective Adventures*, pp. 124–25.

25. *Private Road*, pp. 169–79.

26. *Ibid.*, pp. 179, 68.

27. Anon., review, *Spectator*, CXVIII (January 13, 1917), 49.

28. Anon., review, *Times Literary Supplement* (London), November 9, 1916, p. 536.

29. Anon., review, *Nation* (June 28, 1917), 760.

30. Anon., review, New York *Times*, February 11, 1917, p. 51.

31. *Pirates of the Spring* (London, 1919). Intra-text references are to this novel unless otherwise indicated.

32. Burlingham, p. 154.

33. Anon., review, *Times Literary Supplement* (London), March 1, 1920, p. 173.

34. Anon., review, *Nation*, March 6, 1920, p. 305; *Booklist*, April 20, 1920, p. 246.

35. Anon., review, *Springfield Republican*, March 21, 1920, p. 11a.

36. Anon., review, New York *Times*, March 28, 1920, p. 148.

37. *Pender Among the Residents* (London, 1922). Intra-text references are to this novel unless otherwise indicated.

38. Praz, *op. cit.*, p. 208.

39. Killis Campbell, ed., *The Poems of Edgar Allen Poe* (New York, 1962), p. 63.

40. *Ibid.*, p. 117.

41. Anon., review, New York *Times*, February 4, 1923, p. 16.

42. Anon., review, *Times Literary Supplement* (London), November 16, 1922, p. 746.

43. *Private Road*, pp. 192–93.

44. *Ibid.*, p. 60.

Chapter Five

1. *Demophon: A Traveller's Tale* (London, 1927). Intra-text references are to this novel unless otherwise indicated.

2. Pater, "The Myth of Demeter and Persephone," *Greek Studies*, (London, 1908) pp. 81–151.

3. *Private Road*, p. 198.

4. *Ibid.*

5. John Senior, *The Way Down Out: The Occult in Symbolist Literature* (Ithaca, 1959), p. xxiii.

6. *Ibid.*, p. xxv.

7. *Ibid.*, p. 32.

8. Norman O. Brown, *Hermes the Thief: The Evolution of a Myth* (New York, 1969).

9. A. J. Festugière, *La Révélation d'Hermès Trismégiste* II (Paris, 1949).

10. *Private Road*, p. 198.

11. Burlingham, p. 174.

12. *Uncle Stephen* (London, 1931). Intra-text references are to this novel unless otherwise indicated.

13. *Private Road*, p. 231.

14. *Ibid.*, p. 235.

15. *Uncle Stephen*, Frontispiece.

16. *Private Road*, p. 233.

17. *Brian Westby*, p. 24.

18. F. M. Godfrey, "Forrest Reid," *Time and Tide*, XXVIII, 3 (January 18, 1947), 78.

19. Burlingham, p. 63.

20. Godfrey, *loc. cit.*

21. Anon., review, *Times Literary Supplement* (London), October 29, 1931, p. 838.

22. Liddell, p. 293.

23. *Brian Westby* (London, 1934), Frontispiece. Intra-text references are to this novel unless otherwise indicated.

24. Burlingham, p. 20.

25. Bonamy Dobrée, "Brian Westby," *Spectator* CLII (March 9, 1954), 384.

26. Burlingham, pp. 113–27.

27. John Boyd, "The Achievement of Forrest Reid," *The Dublin Magazine* XIX-XX (July-September, 1945), p. 22.

28. Burlingham, p. 166.

29. *The Retreat*, in *Tom Barber* (New York, 1955). Intra-text references are to this novel unless otherwise indicated.

30. *Ibid.*, p. 158.

31. *Private Road*, p. 239.

32. Edwin Muir, "New Novels," *The Listener*, XV, No. 377 (April 8, 1936), 696.

33. Edward Crankshaw, "New Fiction," *Time and Tide*, XVII, No. 14 (April 4, 1936), 492.

34. *Young Tom*, in *Tom Barber* (New York, 1955). Intra-text references are to this novel unless otherwise indicated.

35. Laura Benet, "Ear to the Unseen," *Saturday Review*, XXXVIII (November 12, 1955), 17.

36. Forster, "Introduction," *Tom Barber* p. 9.

37. Jessamyn West, "Triple Tom," *Spectator*, CLXXXI (October 29, 1955), 367.

38. *Ibid.*

39. Edwin Muir, *The Listener*, XXXII, No. 808 (July 6, 1944), 22.

Chapter Six

1. Edward Wagenknecht, *William Dean Howells; The Friendly Eye* (New York, 1969).

2. Burlingham, p. 212.

3. "Stephen Gooden: An Iconographical Note," in *Retrospective Adventures*, p. 194.

4. *Ibid.*

5. *Ibid.*, p. 196.

6. *Ibid.*

7. "Henry James," *Retrospective Adventures*, p. 87.

8. Forrest Reid, "The Light of the Soul," *Nation and Athenaeum*, XXX (March 11, 1922), 866.

9. "Minor Fiction in the 1880's," *Retrospective Adventures*, p. 67.

10. Percy B. Shelley, "Prometheus Unbound," Act III, ll. 195–98, in David Perkins, *English Romantic Writers* (New York, 1967), p. 1010.

Selected Bibliography

PRIMARY SOURCES
(Chronological Order)

The Kingdom of Twilight. London: T. Fisher Unwin, 1904.

The Garden God: A Tale of Two Boys. London: David Nutt, 1905.

The Bracknels: A Family Chronicle. London: Edward Arnold, 1911.

Following Darkness. London: Edward Arnold, 1912.

The Gentle Lover: A Comedy of Middle Age. London: Edward Arnold, 1913.

W. B. Yeats: A Critical Study. London: Martin Secker, 1915; New York: Dodd, Mead and Co., 1915; New York: Haskell House, 1972.

At the Door of the Gate. London: Edward Arnold, 1915; Boston and New York: Houghton Mifflin Co., 1916.

The Spring Song. London: Edward Arnold, 1916; Boston and New York: Houghton Mifflin Co., 1917.

A Garden by the Sea: Stories and Sketches. Dublin: The Talbot Press, 1918; London: T. Fisher Unwin, 1918.

Pirates of the Spring. Dublin: The Talbot Press, 1919; London: T. Fisher Unwin, 1919; Boston and New York: Houghton Mifflin Co., 1920; Michigan: Scholarly Press, 1971.

Pender Among the Residents. London: W. Collins Sons & Co., 1922; Boston and New York: Houghton Mifflin Co., 1923; Michigan: Scholarly Press, 1971.

Apostate. London: Constable & Co., 1926; Boston and New York: Houghton Mifflin Co., 1926; a reissue of this book, without alteration, was published in London: Faber and Faber, 1947.

Demophon: A Traveller's Tale. London: W. Collins Sons & Co., 1927.

Illustrators of the Sixties. London: Faber & Gwyer, 1928; New York: Dover Press, 1975.

Walter de la Mare: A Critical Study. London: Faber and Faber, [1929]; New York: Henry Holt and Co., n. d. [1929]; Michigan: Scholarly Press, 1970. Reprint of 1929 edition.

Uncle Stephen. London: Faber and Faber, 1931. A German edition, *Onkel*

Stephen, was translated by Hans R. Dufour, Braunschweig: Löwen-Verlag GmbH. 1947.

Brian Westby. London: Faber and Faber, 1934; Toronto: Ryerson Press, 1934. The Ryerson Press acted as Canadian representatives of Faber and Faber.

The Retreat; or, The Machinations of Henry. London: Faber and Faber, 1936; Toronto: Ryerson Press, 1936.

Peter Waring. London: Faber and Faber, 1937; Toronto: Ryerson Press, 1937; South Belfast: Blackstaff Press, 1976.

Private Road. London: Faber and Faber, 1940; Toronto: Ryerson Press, 1940.

Retrospective Adventures. London: Faber and Faber, 1941; Toronto: Ryerson Press, 1941.

Notes and Impressions. Newcastle, Co. Down: The Mourne Press, 1942.

Poems from the Greek Anthology trans. by Forrest Reid. London: Faber and Faber, 1943.

Young Tom; or, Very Mixed Company. London: Faber and Faber, 1944. A German edition, *Der Kleine Tom, oder, Sehr Gemischte Gesellschaft* was translated by Friedrich Wall, Braunschweig: Löwen-Verlag GmbH., 1947.

The Milk of Paradise: Some Thoughts on Poetry. London: Faber and Faber, 1946.

Denis Bracknel. London: Faber and Faber, 1947.

Tom Barber (Young Tom, The Retreat, Uncle Stephen). New York: Pantheon Books Inc., 1955. This trilogy is a reprint of Reid's three novels, hitherto published singly.

SECONDARY SOURCES

1. *Books*

BELL, SAM HANNA, ed. *The Arts in Ulster: A Symposium.* London: George G. Harrap, 1951. In a chapter entitled "Ulster Prose," John Boyd finds Reid a unique figure in his own rather limited field, whose achievement is "an assured one in modern literature." He compares *Apostate* to Aksakoff's *Years of Childhood,* briefly traces Reid's ability as a writer to *Demophon* and the *Tom Barber* trilogy, dicusses his visionary qualities and his difference from "A. E." (George Russell) in their approach to literature, comments on the fusion of Mediterranean and Celtic elements in a writer whose roots were deep in Ulster, and compares Reid's portrayal of children to Joyce Cary's novel *A House of Children* for the discipline and restraint evident in the prose of both.

BOYD, ERNEST. *Ireland's Literary Renaissance.* New York: Alfred Knopf, 1922. Praises Reid's ability to convey the Celtic feeling for the spiritual beauty of nature revealed in an excellent prose style, and his faithful rendering of Northern Irish conditions comparable only to the plays of Rutherford Mayne.

BRYAN, MARY C. "Forrest Reid and the Greek World: A Study of His Novels." Ann Arbor, Michigan: University Microfilms, 1959, No. 3454. Critical study of the novels of Forrest Reid that shows the extent to which the antique shaped and formed the vision of his novels.

BURLINGHAM, RUSSELL. *Forrest Reid: A Portrait and a Study.* London: Faber and Faber, 1953. First full-length critical study of Reid; reveals his personality, individualism, style, technique, and the art of his five major novels. An important book for an understanding of Reid the man as a short-story writer, novelist, autobiographer, and critic.

DE LA MARE, WALTER. *Behold, This Dreamer!* New York: Alfred Knopf, 1939. In this anthology of poems and of passages in prose on dreams and imagination, de la Mare includes Reid with Stevenson, J. A. Symonds, William Hutton, Lafcadio Hearn, and J. Middleton Murray who have a sense of the "day long haunting foreboding of what night and sleep will bring." Also quotes a passage from *Apostate* on night dreams and Reid's fear as a child of going to sleep in an unfriendly house.

Dictionary of Irish Writers. Comp. Brian Cleeve. 1st ser. Cork: Mercier Press, 1967. Factual listing of Reid's works; unfortunately, lacks even a hint of his essential literary qualities.

The Dictionary of National Biography, 1941–50. Ed. L. G. Wickham Legg and E. T. Williams. New York: Oxford University, 1959. Brief factual account of Reid's family background, chronology of his novels and criticism, his autobiography, and his life interests and accomplishments.

ELLIS, S. M. *Mainly Victorian.* London: Hutchinson and Co., 1924. Ellis goes beyond those usually considered Victorian and includes Sheila Kaye-Smith, Alec Waugh, and Forrest Reid who, though born prior to 1901, the year of Queen Victoria's death, were the young generation of novelists.

FORSTER, E. M. *Abinger Harvest.* New York: Meridian Press, 1955. Discusses Reid as a Belfast novelist who has captured the squalor of the city and the beauty of its environs by blending the supernatural and the ethical into his visionary novels on the subject of youth.

———. *Two Cheers for Democracy.* New York: Arnold, 1951. In a chapter on his friend Reid after his death, Forster describes his gentleness, his love for animals, his passionate feeling for Northern Ireland that was not political, his respect for Henry James, his literary association with de la Mare, and his belief in the importance of the past, a characteristic they both shared.

GILBERT, STEPHEN. *Forrest Reid Memorial.* Foxton, England: Burlington Press, 1952, pp. 11–12; rpt. in *A Library of Literary Criticism: Modern*

British Literature. comp. and ed. by R. Z. Temple and M. Tucker, III (1966), 18–22. Assesses Reid's art in his portrayal of typical Ulster characters from the middle classes, both upper and lower, as well as "lapsed" aristocrats. Points up Reid's affinities with ancient Greece and Renaissance Italy as being not at all unusual, since both countries have much in common. This volume also contains a selection from E. M. Forster's *Abinger Harvest* that stresses the visionary, ethical, and stylistic characteristics of Reid as a novelist; a short quotation by Walter de la Mare from the *Forrest Reid Memorial* on Reid as an artist whose memories haunt one of his "loveliest and wisest" of books, *The Milk of Paradise;* and a selection from V. S. Pritchett's criticism of the background of *Peter Waring*, which he compared to Turgenev's Russia. Pritchett highlights Reid's uniqueness when he says that "there is no living writer in English who can describe growing boyhood" as Reid does. A final selection from Russell Burlingham's *Forrest Reid* discusses Reid's critical approach to imaginative literature with his emphasis on the importance of art for beauty's sake in his esthetic.

GWYNN, STEPHEN. *Irish Literature and Drama in the English Language.* New York: Thomas Nelson and Sons, 1936. A lament that the Irish Academy of Letters should be so "imperfectly representative" of the life of Ulster except for the original membership of Forrest Reid, whose novels and short stories of Belfast life are distinguished by a special feeling for nature.

LIDDELL, ROBERT. "Intimations of Immortality." In *Robert Liddell on the Novel.* Chicago: University of Chicago Press, 1969. In the "Appendix" to his study, Liddell links Marcel Proust, Henri Fournier, and Forrest Reid in a spiritual vision of life. Special section on Reid relates him to Wordsworth, explores *Apostate* briefly, and discusses the relationship of dream to creativity in several of Reid's novels. Excellent beginning study for students.

RICHTER, ANNE J., ed. *Literary Prizes and Their Winners.* New York: R. Bowker Co., 1946, pp. 81–83. History of literary prizes and their recipients that includes the James Tait Black Memorial Prize recipients from 1919. Forrest Reid received this award in 1944 for *Young Tom*, judged to be the best work of fiction in that year.

STONE, WILFRED. *The Cave and the Mountain: A Study of E. M. Forster.* Stanford, California: Stanford University Press, 1966. In a scholarly study of Forster, Stone, by juxtaposing Reid and Cavafy, reveals a bias that limits his understanding of Reid's artistic qualities in general as he fails to see why Forster praised Reid's work so highly.

TINDALL, WILLIAM YORK. *Forces in Modern British Literature.* New York: Vintage Press, 1956. Mentions Reid's critical study of Walter de la Mare (1929); in his discussion of the novels of adolescence, lists Reid's *Peter Waring* (1937) with Rolland's *Jean Christophe* (Eng. tr. 1910),

Stephen Spender's *The Backward Son* (1940), and Jack Common's *The Ampersand* (1954), among others.

Twentieth Century Authors. Ed. Stanley J. Kunitz and Howard Haycraft. New York: H. W. Wilson Co., 1942. Also, Stanley J. Kunitz and Vineta Colby, eds., 1st supplement (New York, 1955), p. 820. Brief entry discusses Reid as a notable English stylist and as a "pronounced romanticist" whose novels of children and adolescents are successful studies in "abnormal psychology."

WAGENKNECHT, EDWARD. *As Far as Yesterday: Memories and Reflections.* Norman: University of Oklahoma Press, 1968. In this autobiography, Professor Wagenknecht has a fascinating chapter entitled "Vale: Books—The Real Time Machines" in which he discusses the influence of J. W. Dunne's serial time concepts on the production of novels and plays concerned with time traveling, including Reid's *Uncle Stephen*.

————. *Cavalcade of the English Novel.* New York: Henry Holt and Co., 1954. In a succinct discussion of Reid the individualist Professor Wagenknecht reveals the personality and the mind informing his fiction as well as the influences that shaped his imagination. He also points out the relationship between de la Mare, Reid, and Blake.

————, ed. *The Fireside Book of Ghost Stories.* Indianapolis: Bobbs-Merrill Co., 1946. In an unusual anthology of ghost stories, rather than terror or supernatural tales, the critical introduction sets the tone for the harvest of stories classified as "fantasy, sometimes symbolic . . . written ostensibly for children but also read with avidity by adults." For the larger issues that these stories contain as they extend the human horizon beyond the limits of realism and naturalism, Edward Wagenknecht includes Reid's tale "Courage," a strangely haunting story of psychic experience.

————, ed. *When I Was a Child.* New York: E. P. Dutton, 1946. In an excellent anthology of classic fragments of autobiography—American, British, and Irish—with a critical introduction by Walter de la Mare that sets the tone of the volume, Professor Wagenknecht includes Forrest Reid's "Looking Back through Time," an excerpt from *Apostate*.

WEYGANDT, CORNELIUS. *A Century of the English Novel.* New York: D. Appleton-Century Co., 1925. In a chapter on the "Neo-Georgians," Weygandt's statement that Reid was as great a sinner as Hugh Walpole in his "exploitation of childhood" needs to be reexamined in the light of Robert Liddell's judgment that in Reid's work, no less than in Proust's or in Alain-Fournier's, his talent bears witness to something permanent in human nature, a desire for a true spiritual country that each creates according to his needs. For Reid's purpose the exploration of reality through the mind of a child or an adolescent is the technique used to explore "the other."

2. *Articles*

BENET, LAURA. "Ear to the Unseen." *Saturday Review*, XXXVIII
(November 12, 1955), 17. Analyzes the penetrating quality of Reid's
genius in the *Tom Barber* trilogy by his fusion of fantasy and reality.
Relates him to Mark Twain and Thomas Bailey Aldridge in his creation
of immortal boy heroes.

BOYD, ERNEST. "Pipes of Pan in Belfast," *New York Tribune*, June 11,
1922, p. 4. Boyd briefly discusses Reid's novels as far as *Pirates of the
Spring*, the Romantic Realism of his short stories, and his Celtic feeling
for the spiritual beauty in nature.

BOYD, JOHN. "The Achievement of Forrest Reid." *Dublin Magazine*,
XIX-XX (July-September, 1945), 18–24. Perceptive evaluation of
Reid's achievement; stresses the importance of *Apostate* and *Private
Road* as "the key to the man and his achievement." Sees Reid as a
Romantic on whom the influence of Greek thought is evident through-
out his writings. Defines Reid as "preeminently an explorer into the
mind and spirit of youth" whose acceptance of the limitations of his
range gave a focus to his work.

———. "Forrest Reid: An Introduction to his Work." *Irish Writing*, No. 4
(April, 1948), 72–77. In a brief analysis of Reid's accomplishment as an
outstanding prose stylist, Boyd discusses *The Bracknels*, *Following
Darkness* (rewritten as *Peter Waring*), *Demophon*, and *Apostate*. He
comments on Reid's stylistic qualities, which place him in the tradition
of comparable European writers whose subject is youth. Then he ranks
him with Goldsmith in the eighteenth century and E. M. Forster and
Anatole France among the moderns—all writers who make "the art of
prose narrative seem child's play."

B[RYSON], J. N. B. "Obituary Notice." London *Times*, January 11, 1947, p.
7. Pays tribute to Reid's "exquisite evocations of childhood" which ring
true because of his mastery of literary craft and style that insures him a
place among English novelists.

B[UCHANAN], G. H. P. "Writer of Vision and Delicacy." London *Times*,
January 7, 1947, p. 7. Praises Reid's ability to sustain point of view, to
express a "spring-like freshness," and to render a mystical and dream
quality through his use of the pastoral tradition. Notes that his work is
closer to contemporary history in Ulster than has been previously sup-
posed.

CRANKSHAW, EDWARD. "New Fiction." *Time and Tide*, XVII, No. 14 (April
4, 1936), 492. Among other writers of fiction, Crankshaw singles out
Reid as a "novelist of genius and complete maturity" whose *The Retreat*
is an exceptional novel about his hero's inner conflict when "adolescence comes to tear him out of childhood."

DOBRÉE, BONAMY. "Brian Westby." *Spectator*, CLII (March 9, 1954), 384.
Extols Reid's ability to write in the French tradition of "having a story

and sticking to it"; criticizes his failure to use words to convey ideas that have "the reality of actual life."

ELLIS, S. M. "Forrest Reid." *Bookman,* LVIII ([London] May, 1920), 65–66. Discusses Reid's ability to portray the natural landscape of the wild seacoast and the Mourne mountains symbolized in his use of the benevolent Pan. Points out his Celtic qualities fused with "the Greek belief in inevitable fate" and briefly analyzes each novel through *Pirates of the Spring.* On the plane of the supernatural romance, he finds Reid's chief strength.

GILBERT, STEPHEN. "Forrest Reid—the Man." *School News,* Royal Belfast Academical Institution, LV (Easter, 1947), 55–57. Gilbert pays tribute to Reid as a great man whose genius was unrecognized in Ulster. The personality of Reid lives in this friendly account of his memories of Reid as a conversationalist, his understanding of human character and motives, his hatred of lies, his contempt for those who compromised with their consciences, his ability to relate to children and animals, his willingness to help other writers, and the enthusiasm with which he reviewed books. Gilbert judges Reid to be "the only Ulsterman who ever made a considerable contribution to British literature."

GODFREY, F. M. "Forrest Reid." *Time and Tide,* XXVIII (January 18, 1947), 78. Lauds Reid as a confessional writer distinguished by his natural beauty of style and the "innate humanism of his mind" in his explorations of the world through the eyes of a child. Rarely, he comments, has there been such a close union of a "dream-creation with autobiographical reality." Godfrey sees as well as feels Reid's affinity for nature which derives from the Greeks, his feeling for the concrete, and the poetical character of his prose.

HEWITT, JOHN. "Some Notes on Writing in Ulster." *The Bell,* XVIII (July, 1952), 197–202. Places Reid among those Irish writers who preferred to "rarefy" rather than to court popular success; includes Reid with Stephen Gilbert, Michael McLaverty, and John O'Connor whose stay with the lyrical mode limits their reading audience. Hewitt's preference for the Zola-Flaubert schools conditions and limits his appreciation of the poetic novel.

LYND, ROBERT. "Forrest Reid." *School News,* Royal Belfast Academical Institution, LV (Easter, 1947), 57–58. Testimonial to Reid from a fellow classmate; recalls Reid as a loner at school and at a champion croquet tournament at Hampstead in the company of de la Mare and E. M. Forster. As a novelist of imaginative boyhood, Lynd describes Reid as "the most sensitive and delicate artist that has yet appeared in our Province." The subtlety of his style "will always appeal chiefly to the adult reader."

MUIR, EDWIN. "New Novels." *The Listener,* XV, No. 377 (April 8, 1936), 696. In evaluating the literary qualities of the *Tom Barber* trilogy, Muir

captures the serenity, quietness, and ease of Reid's tone which culminated in *Young Tom*, "one of the most original and most perfect works
of imagination of his time."

O'HEGARTY, P. S. "About Ulster Novelists." *The Bell*, IV (July, 1942), 293.
Evaluates Reid's contribution to literary criticism in *Retrospective Adventures* especially evident in the Irish essays and "Minor Fiction in
the Eighteen-Eighties." Finds Reid's criticism of Henry James, Emily
Brontë, and Arthur Rimbaud more a study of personality than of their
works.

SPARROW, JOHN (The Honorable). "Forrest Reid." Typescript radio talk
delivered over the Third Programme, British Broadcasting Company,
February 1, 1947. In his talk, Sparrow captures what Yeats called "the
distress of boyhood changing into man" in a natural easy manner so
evident in Reid's fiction. He suggests a comparison of Reid's novels
with Dickens's *David Copperfield* and Proust's *Swann's Way*. Stylistically, he compares Reid to Max Beerbohm in their excellent use of the
English language by quoting passages from *Apostate*.

WAGENKNECHT, EDWARD. "The Little Prince Rides the White Deer: Fantasy and Symbolism in Recent Literature." *College English*, VII (May,
1946), 431–37. In a provocative, scholarly essay, Professor
Wagenknecht discusses the abundance of fantasy literature for adult
reading in the 1940's, concurrent with "the most unnecessary war in
history." In noting the meaning of this phenomenon, he mentions
Marjorie Bowen and Forrest Reid, whose use of the psychic and the
supernatural is as natural to them as "the minutiae of life in Gopher
Prairie" is to other novelists.

WEST, GEOFFREY, ed. "The Artist and the World Today." *Bookman* (London), LXXXVI (May, 1934), 92–93. Against the implications of questions in this symposium that imply that relevance makes art, Reid
placed his dedication to imaginative literature squarely on the line by
reference to Homer's *Odyssey* and Shakespeare's *A Midsummer
Night's Dream* which have less to do with existing conditions than with
the creative imagination working at its highest level.

WEST, JESSAMYN. "Triple Tom." *Spectator*, CLXXXI (October 29, 1955),
367. Tries hard to explain Virginia Woolf's refusal to give Reid a chance
by suggesting that Woolf may have thought that Tom, like his creator,
was not interested in maturity, but the defense fails to be convincing.
Otherwise, West finds Reid humorless (which is rather amazing) but
grants that the strength of *Uncle Stephen* comes from the universality
of its theme and from the pleasure of this "fresh and honest book."

Index

Aksakoff, Ivan, 33
Alain-Fournier, 33, 39, 127
Allen, Grant, 85
Anderson, Sherwood, 149
Animism, 20, 21, 38, 39, 40, 59, 99, 102, 121, 123–24, 134, 139
American Civil War, 17
Apollodorus, 139
Apollonius of Tyana, 125
Apostles Club, 25
Apuleius, 85, 89
Arnold, Matthew, 35, 47
Asceticism, 41
Austen, Jane, 34

Bass Rock, 17
Baudelaire, Charles, 56
Belfast (environs), 16, 17, 19, 24, 30, 90, 104, 144
Benet, Laura, 142, 165
Bennett, Arnold, 148
Benson, E. F.: *David Blaize*, 108
Benson, Stella, 33
Berenson, Bernard, 85
Bergman, Ingmar, 42
Bible, The (allusions to): Cain and Abel, 90, 91, 92, 93, 94; Jacob, 93; Job, 121; Jonathan and David, 61; Saint Paul, 41, 95
Blake, William, 35, 46, 115, 132, 138
Blavatsky, Madame Elena, 36
Bookman, The (London), 32
Botticelli, 87
Boyd, Ernest, 165–66
Boyd, John, 132, 162, 166
Bridges, Robert, 49

Brontë, Emily, 30, 33, 47, 49 (*Wuthering Heights*), 145, 148
Brooke, Rupert, 26
Broughton, Rhoda, 19, 72
Browning, Robert: "Porphyro's Lover," 93
Bruges, 84, 85, 87, 89, 144
Bryson, J. N., 31
Buchanan, George, 31
Burlingham, Russell, 15, 27, 37, 48, 107, 127, 130–31, 132, 146, 147
Butler, Samuel: *The Way of All Flesh*, 74, 130

Caird, Edward, 23, 81
Camus, Albert, 43
Carlyle, Thomas, 46
Carroll, Lewis (Charles Dodgson): *Alice in Wonderland*, 50
Catholicism, Roman, 39, 86, 107
Cavafy, Constantin, 37
Censorship Bill, 15, 28
Chatterton, Thomas, 27
Christianity, 15, 18, 19, 20, 35, 41, 45, 59, 75, 85, 87, 124, 125, 129, 130
Coleridge, Samuel Taylor, 30, 35, 46, 111
Collins, Wilkie, 33
Colum, Padraic, 26, 85
Conrad, Joseph, 33, 41, 42, 146, 148
Crankshaw, Edward, 136, 166

D'Annunzio, Gabriele, 33, 60
de la Mare, Walter, 15, 23, 28, 30, 31, 33, 46, 48, 51–53 (*Memoirs of a Midget*); 51 (*The Return*); 50–51 (*The*

Three Mulla-Mulgars); 90, 102, 145, 146, 148, 150, 163
Demeter, 18, 29, 38, 51, 115, 116, 120
de Selincourt, Basil, 28, 70, 94, 102
Dickens, Charles, 24, 33
Dionysian, 58
Dionysius, 61, 63
Dobrée, Bonamy, 130
Donne, John, 95
Douglas, Norman: *Birds and Beasts of the Greek Anthology*, 102
Dowson, Ernest, 55
Dreams, 42–43, 56, 62, 63, 75, 79, 123, 145, 149, 150; dream technique, 131, 133, 134–35
Dunne, J. W., 43

Eleusinian mysteries, 36; Eleusis, 144
Eliot, George (Mary Ann Evans), 85
Eliot, Thomas Stearns, 37, 100
Ellis, S. M., 166–67
Emerson, Ralph Waldo, 43
Epicurus, 41, 65
Euripides, 49

Fabian Society, 36
Festugiere, A. J., 116
Firbank, Ronald, 25–26
Flaubert, Gustave: *Madame Bovary*, 78; 88, 146
Forster, Edward Morgan, 26, 27 (*Maurice*), 28, 30, 32, 33, 45 (*Two Cheers for Democracy*), 71, 133, 142–43, 150
France, Anatole, 31, 33, 37, 41, 50, 65, 81
Frazer, Sir James G., 139
Freedman, Ralph, 47, 48
Freemasonry, 36
Freud, Sigmund, 43

Garden (imagery), 64, 65
Garnett, Richard, 30, 35
Ghandi, 45
Gide, André: *Strait is the Gate*, 21; 27, 33
Gilbert, Stephen: *The Landslide*, 31, 128, 163, 167; 37
Godfrey, F. M., 127, 167

Gollancz, Israel, 25
Gooden, Stephen, 147
Gorky, Maxim: *My Childhood*, 148
Gosse, Edmund, 27, 33, 79
Grahame, Kenneth, 44, 154n58
Greece, 18, 19, 34–35, 36, 37, 38, 59, 61, 65, 70, 87, 114, 116, 124–25, 129, 145, 149
Greek: Themes in literature (myth), 41, 62, 63, 64, 65, 75, 85, 90, 92, 95–96, 99, 107, 110–11, 112, 115, 128, 129, 140, 141, 145; painting, 42, 84, 87; sculpture, 42, 61, 63, 64, 89, 92, 116, 122, 123; world view, 130, 139, 140
Greek Anthology, The, 37, 95, 115
Greeves, Arthur, 31
Gwynn, Stephen, 164

Hall, G. Stanley, 78
Hamsun, Knut: *The Wanderer*, 148
Hardy, Thomas: *Jude the Obscure*, 46, 60; 47, 78 (*Tess of the D'Ubervilles*)
Hart, J. N., 30
Hebraism, 35, 39
Hellenic, 32, 36, 89; Hellenism, 35, 36, 37, 43, 45, 54, 89; Hellenist (Romantic), 36, 150; Hellenists, 45
Heraclitus, 43
Hergerscheimer, Joseph: *The Bright Shawl*, 149
Hermes, 22, 29, 42, 115 passim, 125, 140; cult of, 29; of Praxiteles, 22, 42
Hermetic Order of the Golden Dawn, 36, 49
Hesse, Herman, 33, 43, 44; (*Demian*), 60, 65
Hewitt, John, 167
Holmes, Emma, 18, 29, 115
Homer, 37
Homeric Hymns, 21, 22
Howells, William Dean, 146, 148, 149
Hudson, W. H., 30, 33, 148
Hughes, Arthur, 28, 147
Hugo, Victor, 19
Humanism, 20, 24, 35, 38, 41, 45, 59, 84, 85, 86, 87, 88, 89, 124–25, 129, 130; Humanistic values, 32, 114, 115
Huysman, Joris, Karl: *Là-Bas*, 56
Hyde, Douglas, 151n5

Ireland, S. J., 33
Irish Literary Renaissance, 24
Irish Statesman, The, 28

James, Henry, 27, 30, 31, 33, 60, 65, 69 ("The Pupil"), 83, 84, 89, 101, 148 *(The Awkward Age)*
Jeffries, Richard: *Bevis,* 149
Johnson, Samuel, 41
Joyce, James: *A Portrait of the Artist,* 33, 74

Keats, John, 35, 111
Keene, Charles, 147
Klingopoulos, G. D., 45

Le Fanu, Joseph Sheridan, 33
Liddell, Robert, 127
Livingstone, R. W., 38, 41
Lynd, Robert, 19, 31, 167

McBurney, John, 41
Macaulay, Rose, 48
Macaulay, Thomas B., 136
Macdonald, George: *At the Back of the North Wind; Dealing with Fairies; The Princess and the Goblin,* 147
MacDonnell, Anne, 78
Machen, Arthur, 33
Mackenzie, Compton: *Sinister Street,* 33, 71, 78
Maeterlinck, Maurice: *The Bluebird,* 49
Mallarméism, 49
Manchester Guardian, 28, 78
Mann, Thomas, 33, 65 *(Death in Venice),* 75 *(Joseph and His Brothers)*
Mansfield, Katherine, 148
Mather, Helen: *Coming Through the Rye,* 19
Mathers, Macgregor, 49
Maugham, Somerset: "Arabesque," 48; *Of Human Bondage,* 74
Mauriac, François, 29
Melville, Herman, 33
Memlinc, 87
Merimée, Prosper, 110, 111
Mermaid Society, The, 26
Mill, John Stuart: *Autobiography,* 47
Milton, John, 75, 136, 138

Moore, George, 146, 147 *(The Brook Kerith)*
Mozart, Wolfgang, 27
Muir, Edwin, 136, 143, 167

Nashe, Thomas, 95
Nathan, Robert: *Portrait of Jenny,* 126
Nation, The (London), 69
Nation and Athenaeum, 148
Notes and Impressions, 26

O'Hegarty, P. S., 167–68
O'Kelley, Seumas, 30, 47, 145
Ovid, 115

Paley, William, 25
Pann, 22, 39, 42, 43, 54, 62, 63, 76, 95, 117, 140
Parr, Katherine, 18
Pater, Walter, 33, 35, 42, 47–48, 55, 60, 62 ("Flavian"), 65 ("The Child in the House"), 85, 87–88 ("Hippolytus Veiled"), 115 ("The Myth of Demian and Persephone")
Perry, Robin, 31
Peruzzi, Gian, 95
Phillpot, Eden: *The River,* 24
Pindar, 40
Plato, 31, 37, 40–41, 55, 58, 63, 64; Platonism, 38, 61; Platonist, 76
Poe, Edgar Allen: "Ulalume," 19, 112, 123, "The Sleeper," 19, 110, "The Bells," 137
Proust, Marcel, 33, 127
Pryce, Richard: *Christopher,* 108
Pythagoras, 125

Quigley, James, 21

Raffalovitch, André, 27, 29
Raile, Arthur Lyon (Edward Perry Warren), 30, 145
Realism, 147
Reid, Forrest: ancestry and parentage, 16, 17, 18; apprenticeship, 21; birth, 16; circle of friends, 21, 22–23, 30, 31; compared with E. M. Forster, 45, Walter de la Mare, 48; death, 31, 141; education: Cambridge University,

24–25, Miss Hardy's School, 19, Royal Academical Institution, 19; influence of Classics and Romance, 19, 21; influence of Hellenism. *See* Hellenic; honors, 31; impressions of Cambridge, 25–26; quarrel with Christianity, 19, 20; rejection of creedal religion, 19, 20. *See* Christianity; Socratic Humanism. *See* Humanism and Socrates; theory of creativity, 34, 35; travels, 26, 30; violence, attitude toward, 45; war, attitude toward, 33, 34, 45

WORKS—AUTOBIOGRAPHY:

Apostate, 15, 16, 17, 18, 19, 23, 29, 62, 70, 115, 122

Private Road, 15, 16, 22, 24, 25, 26, 27, 28, 29, 30, 36, 42, 102, 144

WORKS—CRITICISM:

Art: *Illustrators of the Sixties*, 28, 147

Literary: Book Reviews, 28, 35, 146

Milk of Paradise, The, 30, *46–47*

Notes and Impressions, 26

Retrospective Adventures, 26, 30, 33, 47, 145

Walter de la Mare: A Critical Study, 28, *50–53*

W. B. Yeats. A Critical Study, 26, 47, *49–50*

WORKS—NOVELS:

At the Door of the Gate, 28, *89–95*

Bracknels, The. A Family Chronicle, 27, *65–70*. *See Denis Bracknel*

Brian Westby, 30, 42, 114, *127–32*, 142, 145

Demophon: A Traveller's Tale, 18, 29, 38, 114, *115–21*, 145

Denis Bracknel (posthumous publication), *69–70*, 144, 145, 150. *See The Bracknels*

Following Darkness, 28, 33, *71–82*, 107, 145. *See Peter Waring*

Garden God, The, 24, 25, *26–27*, 42, *61–65*, 144

Gentle Lover, The. A Comedy of Middle Age, 28, *83–89*, 90

Kingdom of Twilight, The, 24, 27, 36, 40, *54–61*, 144, 150

Pender Among the Residents, 25, 28, 83, *108–13*

Peter Waring, 28, 40, *79–82*, 145. *See Following Darkness*

Pirates of the Spring, 28, *103–108*

Retreat, The; or, The Machinations of Henry, 30, 114, *132–36*, 142, 145

Spring Song, The, 28, *95–103*, 145, 147

Uncle Stephen, 30, 32, 42–43, 114, *121–27*

Young Tom; or, Very Mixed Company, 30, 31, 32, 36, 42–43, 114, *136–43*, 145, 146

WORKS—SHORT STORIES:

Garden by the Sea, A, 20

"Pan's Pupil," in *Ulad*, 24

WORKS—TRANSLATIONS:

Poems from the Greek Anthology, 30

Reynolds, W. B., 24

Rimbaud, Arthur, 30, 146

Rilke, Reiner Maria, 115

Robinson, Master Romney, 30, 112, 113

Rodenbach, Georges: *Bruges-La Morte*, 84

Romanticism, 64

Rosicrucian Society, 36

Rossetti, Dante Gabriel, 28, 147

Russell, George ("A. E."), 26, 35, 102

Rutherford, Andrew, 21, 22–23, 26, 30

Rutherford, James, 25, 27, 30

Rutherford, Mark (William Hale White), 23 *(Autobiography)*, 91, 95

Saint Augustine, 43

Saint Paul, 41, 95

Sappho, 58

Schreiner, Olive, 33, 145, 148

Seferis, George, 37

Shakespeare, William, 71, 72, 79, 146–47

Shelley, Percy Bysshe, 35, 46, 48, 71, 79, 150

Skeat, W. W., 25, 113

Society for Psychical Research, 26, 36, 39

Socrates, 20, 22, 27, 40–41, 126, 130

Socratic philosophy, 95, 126

Sophocles, 37, 49
Sparrow, The Hon. John, 168
Spencer, Herbert, 23, 76, 80, 81
Spinario, 42, 62, 63
Spiritualism, 86
Stevenson, Robert Louis, 33
Stone, Wilfred, 45
Sturgis, Harold: *Tim*, 27
Sullivan, Arthur, 137–38
Swedenborg, Emmanuel, 115
Symons, Arthur, 47, 65, 115
Synge, John Millington, 35
Symbolists, 55; Symbolist movement, 115

Taylor, Jeremy, 50
Terence, 44
Thacheray, William M., 34, 49 (*Vanity Fair*)
Theocritus, 21, 37, 40, 43, 55, 59, 107, 125
Thomas, Dylan, 44
Time and Tide, 136
Times (New York), 112
Times Literary Supplement (London), 95, 127
Tindall, William York, 74
Tolkien, J. R. R., 33
Tolstoy, Leo, 75, 149
Trilling, Lionel, 45
Turgenev, Ivan, 33, 61 (First Love), 156–11

Twain, Mark (Samuel Clemens), 54, 149 (*Huckleberry Finn*)

Ulad, 24
Ulster, 15, 18, 31, 83, 84; Ulster Renaissance, 24
Utopia, 44, 145

Vaughan, Henry, 110, 132
Verlaine, Paul, 55

Wagenknecht, Edward, 15, 146, 165, 168
Walpole, Hugh: *Jeremy*, 108
Watson, John Dawson, 28
West, Geoffrey, 168
West, Jessamyn, 143, 168
Weygandt, Cornelius, 165
Woolf, Virginia, 33, 142–43, 146 (*Jacob's Room*), 148
Wordsworth, William, 35, 47, 91, 94, 95, 102, 121, 126, 132
Workman, Reverend Frank, 27
Workman, Mrs. Frank, 31

Yakovnin, 127–28
Yeats, W. B., 24, 31, 35, 46–47, 53, 145, 148

Zeller, Eduard, 92